D1260451

CANADIAN HISTORICAL DOCUMENTS SERIES

Volume I

The French Régime

Edited and translated by

CAMERON NISH

PRENTICE-HALL OF CANADA, LTD.
SCARBOROUGH, ONTARIO

Library of Congress Catalog Card No.: 65-23525

71449

PRINTED IN CANADA

C-11315(P)

C-11316(C)

To

EDWARD EASTMAN MCCULLOUGH

and

GUY FRÉGAULT

"Le corps est aussi un absolu."

GATIEN LAPOINTE

Contents

v

Contents

Introduction

The French Régime in Canada: how did it begin? How did it develop? What did it accomplish? One way to answer these questions is to study the documents of the period. This is a book of such documents, a first-hand account by a few of the individuals involved in the founding and settling of Canada during the first centuries of its existence. This is the story of their ambitions, deeds, and frustrations, in their own words. Original documents are the bricks of the historical structure, a basic material required for bridging the gap from the present to the past.

The written record is the remnant of the past: words. However, the orderly arrangement of letters embodies more than mere sounds; words shroud emotions and feelings as well. Imagination is the indispensable mortar required for binding words and feelings in a document. For example, we are told by Jacques Cartier, that gold and diamonds were found in the Saguenay region. The hard, cold fact is that his treasures were worthless quartz and pyrite. Other documents tell us that some Jesuits were cruelly martyred for their faith. Yet words, bare words by themselves, tell but part of the story. A disciplined historical imagination enables us to feel with Cartier his elation and disappointment; to share with the Jesuit mystic his union with his God and to recoil at the physical violence done to his tired and abused body.

Sound evidence, heightened perception, and our insatiable curiosity about ourselves lead to a valuable knowledge of the French Régime in Canada. We can know and understand its institutions, its laws, economy, political values, and religion; its friends, enemies, and its conquest, in

1760, by a foreign power. What the French Régime was explains what the French Canadian fact in Canada today is. For the French Canadian, the link between past and present is well expressed by the title of Lionel Groulx's book *Notre Maître, Le Passé (Our Master, the Past)*.

A book of readings on the French Régime in Canada presents, as do all works involving selection and emphasis, delicate—and possibly controversial—issues which should be squarely faced. Should Columbus and Verrazano be included as the precursors of Cartier and Champlain? Are the English settlements of Newfoundland and Nova Scotia part of the French Régime? Or do they more properly belong to the history of British America? Were the explorations of Cartier, Champlain, and the host of intrepid young men who ventured into the unknown continent an end in themselves or were they but means to other ends? Was the seigniorial régime, and the seigniorial class, a feudal institution transferred to a strange milieu or part and parcel of the economy and colonization of New France?

The ultimate resolution of such issues and interpretive predicaments is the formulation of a working axiom: French Canada—more properly speaking, New France—for the purposes of this book of documents, means the Saint Lawrence Valley. The hub of this colonial wheel is the three urban centres of Quebec, Three Rivers, and Montreal. To some extent this is arbitrary. On the other hand Acadia, Ile Royale, the Upper Mississippi, and the hinterlands of the North and West were, to some extent, political, economic, administrative, and religious dependencies of New France. The St. Lawrence Valley is the torso; the dependencies, the limbs of the colonial body.

The deliberate exclusions, and inclusions, serve a very definite purpose. The "romantic" exploits of a "hardy Cartier", or "Champlain's Life of Fortitude", or again the *solely* religious works of the dedicated clergy, men and women, of New France, have been muted. The elements of nation-building, or at least the building of a distinctive *Canadien* society, have been stressed. The links between geographic knowledge, explorations, the Indians, and the missions have been emphasized by including such documents within an integrated interpretation of New France. This less traditional approach, it is hoped, will allow us to know the French Régime in North America through the minds of the inhabitants: to be a *Canadien*, an explorer, a missionary, an administrator, a soldier, and a Catholic all at the same time. This approach leads to a consideration, from the inside, of the relations of the citizens of New France with France, with each other, and with their enemies. It allows us to know, in few words, the *Canadien* context.

For the sake of convenience, and comprehension, the French Régime is divided into four parts, each prefaced by a brief introduction. Within each part the materials are organized by themes and linked by a narrative.

The first, 1534 to 1635, considers early explorations and settlements. The efforts of Cartier and Champlain, the French State, and the Church, as they seek ways and means of erecting a French colony in North America, are the primary problems in this incubatory period of Canadian history.

The era from the death of Champlain to the implementation of Royal Government, 1635 to 1663, indicates a growing awareness on the part of the *Canadiens* and the French of their new milieu. In the period the problems are defined and tentative solutions are put forward.

In the third part, 1663 to 1713, the young colony formalizes the material, political, and social frames which will endure until the conquest of the colony by the English. It is a vigorous and active era dominated by the names of Laval, Talon, and Frontenac.

The time between the Treaty of Utrecht of 1713 and the Capitulation of Montreal in 1760 was notable for success and failure. French Canadian society, as it reached maturity, was active in commerce and agriculture. There was a steady population growth and a developing social sophistication. These were some of the successes. The failure was a little more radical: New France was conquered by the English.

The selection of significant readings for the French Régime of Canadian history was both an easy and a difficult task. There is an abundance of materials, manuscript and printed. In English the *Jesuit Relations*, and Biggar's compilations of the Cartier and Champlain papers, to name but two, provide vast collections to be mined. And many times more material exists in French. This had to be translated. While not difficult, translation is fraught with some pitfalls. A stringent attempt was made to retain the savour and sense of a document, but modern usages were employed. For example, one word, and a simple one at that, is likely to raise the ire of purists. *Sauvage*, literally translated, is *savage*. In many of the documents, however, it is used as a synonym for *Indian*. In the following documents when *sauvage* was used as a noun it was translated as *Indian*; when used in the original document as an adjective it was translated as *savage*. The exceptions to modern usage are the retention of the translation done by others than the editor. Those documents translated by the editor of this book are noted by an asterisk preceding the number of the document.

It will be obvious that the readings in this collection have been vigorously pared. The requirements of space necessitated pruning away unessential words, although it is hoped the original meaning remains undisturbed. Omitted words are always indicated by the ellipsis symbol: ... (* * * for one or more complete paragraphs).

A minor problem in the preparation of this book was the lack of a standard text to which the readings might be correlated. At the moment there is no *one* book that may be used. It is hoped that this lack will be partially overcome by the inclusion of a fairly comprehensive bibliography, and the few appendices giving pertinent information: the reader's attention is drawn particularly to the lists of the Governors, Intendants, Bishops, and Ministers of Marine of the period.

Rapid identification of the source of the document is achieved by the inclusion, by short title, of the source following the title of the reading. Further documents on the same topic and secondary works should be consulted as each section is considered by continuous reference to the bibliographies.

PART I

1534-1635

Prior to Cartier's first voyage in 1534, the Eastern seaboard of Canada and the Gulf of St. Lawrence were known to the mariners and fishermen of Europe. However, the land mass of the interior was unexplored. Perhaps the Unknown Continent contained wealthy kingdoms rivalling those of the Aztecs and Incas so recently plundered by the Spanish? Perhaps the strong-flowing River could provide a short route to the fabled East? These very real hopes lured the French to America.

The great expectations of the French, however, were not to go unchallenged. A powerful Spain and an interested Portugal had vested interests in the Americas: the rights of discovery and occupation, and the Pope's grandiose settlement of the Treaty of Tordesillas of 1494, placed the early explorations and settlements in Canada within an international context. European antagonisms and colonial rivalries are evident even in this early era of Canadian history.

Cartier's two exploratory voyages to the Kingdoms of Stadacona and Hochelaga in 1534 and 1535 revealed not fabulous wealth but rather dingy hovels populated by primitive aborigines. But a third kingdom remained: that of the Saguenay. A settlement was planned with a view to conquering this assuredly wealthy land.

The abject failures of Cartier and Roberval, and unsettled conditions in France, led to a loss of interest in Canada. Then, towards the end of the sixteenth century, interest in Canada quickened. Charters were granted to Aymar de Chastes and Pierre du Guast, Comte de Monts. A

1

settlement was established on St. Croix Island, and later at Port Royal. One of de Monts's employees was Samuel Champlain.

From these permanent bases Champlain ranged up and down the coast of the Atlantic and charted the St. Lawrence inland to what is now Montreal. In 1608, despairing of finding mineral wealth in the Maritimes, or a route to the East, and in order to gain proximity to the sources of furs, Champlain erected a fort at a narrows of the St. Lawrence. Quebec City was founded.

The material and demographic accomplishments of the period were small: there were seventy-six permanent settlers at Quebec in 1628. But Champlain's choice of a site gave a decided cast to Canadian history. The economic and political organization that he advocated, centralized and monopolistic, endured through the whole of the French Régime, and in some ways into the British and Canadian Régimes as well.

While the early hopes of finding wealthy kingdoms or short routes to the East slowly faded, a new economic activity captured and lured the French into the continent. The thick soft pelt of the beaver was found to be a most profitable commodity.

Economic necessity made landlubbers of the French in America and they, in turn, gave a continental mien to Canada. The search for furs entailed an ever-expanding frontier: the St. Lawrence, the Richelieu, Lake Champlain, Georgian Bay, and Lake Ontario were the roads of the continent.

The corollary of a rational exploitation of the fur trade was a sound system of alliances with middlemen: Indians. The Church not only ministered to the spiritual needs of the colonists, but contributed by its proselytizing to the sowing of French influence. The Recollets and Jesuits, in addition to being spiritual funnels, were active agents in exploring and settling the continent in the name of France.

Harsh experience taught the colonists to build sturdy shelters and fortify themselves against unfriendly natives. The frigid winds and sweltering summers taught the French to clothe themselves in a Canadian fashion. Starvation was the result of a poorly-victualled expedition, and the early agriculture of Canada was intimately related to immediate needs.

The requirements of war, trade, and religion compelled the French to learn Indian tongues. The *coureur de bois* learnt to track in snowshoes, live with the Indians, map the interior, manipulate the bark canoe, and encompass the continent for the French.

The small, infant colony, struggling against nature and, often, the indifference of the mother country, faced two other ominous foes: the Iroquois, who would plague the colony for almost a century, and the

English. For a few years, from 1629 to 1632, it appeared as if all were lost. The Kirke brothers captured Quebec, but the French fact in America would survive with the restitution of the colony to France by the Treaty of St. Germain-en-Laye of 1632.

Champlain's death on Christmas Day 1635 is the terminal point of this period. If his reputation were based solely on his cartographic accomplishments, it would be well deserved. However, his contributions were much more significant. The choice of Quebec decided the main path of Canadian history. His writings, and efforts, kept a flagging French interest alive to the potential of Canada. He used the lure of wealth, and the desire for souls, as means to implement his vision of Canada.

A

THE KINGDOMS OF CANADA

The purposes, means, ends, and disputes surrounding early French endeavours in Canada are considered in Documents 1 to 9. The usual means of financing exploratory voyages were charters from the King coupled with some financial aid from the monarch and private individuals. The initial reports submitted by explorers tended to exaggerate both accomplishments and potential, but further assistance was dependent upon extending the truth. Cartier's distribution of gifts to the Indians probably depended somewhat upon how happy he was with the stories they told him. It is only natural that the Indians prevaricated a little and that Cartier chose to be a little credulous. The Spanish and Portuguese feared French ulterior motives. They saw the projected voyages and settlements as means to piracy and rapine and not as Christian projects for the salvation of the souls of the Indians. The Spanish and Portuguese "fifth column" in Europe and America kept their respective courts up to date on French manoeuvres.

*1. "GRANT OF MONEY TO CARTIER FOR HIS FIRST VOYAGE, MARCH 18, 1534" (Biggar, *A Collection of Documents Relating to Jacques Cartier and the Sieur de Roberval*, p. 42).

... the sum of 6,000 livres* tournois ... to pay the necessary costs of the victualling, arming, and equipping ... of ships presently in Brittany, as well as for the pay and training of those who, led by Jacques Cartier, will make the voyage ... to the New Lands to discover ... islands and territories where, it is said, are great quantities of gold and other riches ....

                         PREUDOMME [OF THE MARINE TREASURY]†

2. "CARTIER'S FIRST VOYAGE, 1534" (Biggar, *The Voyages of Jacques Cartier*, pp. 21-23, 49-51, 52-53, 65-67, 79).

... If the soil were as good as the harbours, it would be a blessing; but the land should not be called the New Land, being composed of stones and horrible rugged rocks; for along the whole of the north shore [of the Gulf], I did not see one cart-load of earth and yet I landed in many places. Except at Blanc-Sablon there is nothing but moss and short, stunted shrub. In fine I am rather inclined to believe that this is the land that God gave to Cain. There are people on this coast whose bodies are fairly well formed but they are wild and savage folk. They wear their hair tied up on the top of their heads like a handful of twisted hay, with a nail or something of the sort passed through the middle, and into it they weave a few bird's feathers. They clothe themselves with the furs of animals, both men as well as women; but the women are wrapped up more closely and snuggly in their furs; and have a belt around their waists ....

                              *   *   *

We remained in this cove from [Saturday] the fourth until [Sunday] the twelfth of July. And while there, we set out on Monday, the sixth [of July], after hearing mass, in one of our long-boats, to examine a cape and points of land, that lay seven or eight leagues‡ to the west of us, and to see in which direction the coast ran. And when we were half a league from this point, we caught sight of two fleets of Indian canoes that were crossing from one side [of Chaleur Bay] to the other, which numbered in all some forty or fifty canoes. Upon one of the fleets reaching this

---

* See Appendix F for value of French currency.

† For biographical data on the individuals mentioned in this book see the Reverend Father L. LeJeune's *Dictionnaire Général du Canada* noted in the bibliography on secondary sources.

‡ A measure of distance varying between 2.4 and 4.6 miles. In this instance, the known distance suggests the lower figure as the more accurate.

point, there sprang out and landed a large number of Indians, who set up a great clamour and made frequent signs to us to come on shore, holding up to us some furs on sticks. But as we were only one boat we did did not care to go, so we rowed towards the other fleet which was on the water. And they [on shore], seeing we were rowing away, made ready two of their largest canoes in order to follow us. These were joined by five more of those that were coming in from the sea, and all came after our long-boat, dancing and showing many signs of joy, and of their desire to be friends, saying to us in their language: *Napou tou daman asurtat,** and other words, we did not understand. But for the reason already stated, that we had only one of our long-boats, we did not care to trust to their signs and waved to them to go back, which they would not do but paddled so hard that they soon surrounded our long-boat with their seven canoes. And seeing that no matter how much we signed to them, they would not go back, we shot off over their heads two small cannon. On this they began to return towards the point, and set up a marvellously loud shout, after which they proceeded to come on again as before. And when they had come alongside our long-boat, we shot off two fire-lances which scattered among them and frightened them so much that they began to paddle off in very great haste, and did not follow us any more.

* * *

The next day [Tuesday, July 7] some of these Indians came in nine canoes to the point at the mouth of the cove where we lay anchored with our ships. And being informed of their arrival we went with our two long-boats to the point where they were, at the mouth of the cove. As soon as they saw us they began to run away, making signs to us that they had come to barter with us; and held up some furs of small value, with which they clothe themselves. We likewise made signs to them that we wished them no harm, and sent two men on shore to offer them some knives and other iron goods, and a red cap to give to their chief. Seeing this, they sent on shore part of their people with some of their furs; and the two parties traded together. The savages showed a marvellously great pleasure in possessing and obtaining these iron wares and other commodities, dancing and going through many ceremonies, and throwing salt water over their heads with all hands. They bartered all they had to such an extent that all when back naked without anything on them; and they made signs to us that they would return on the morrow with more furs.

* * *

When we had returned to our ships, the chief dressed in an old black bear-skin, arrived in a canoe with three of his sons and his brother; but they did not come so close to the ships as they had usually done. And pointing to the cross† he [the chief] made us a long harangue, making

---

* Disputes exist as to the exact meaning of this phrase. However, the agreed sense of the words is 'let's be friends'.

† Cartier had erected a cross on Friday, July 24, 1534.

the sign of the cross with two of his fingers; and then he pointed to the land all around about, as if he wished to say that all this region belonged to him, and that we ought not to have set up this cross without his permission. And when he had finished his harangue, we held up an axe to him, pretending we would barter it for his fur-skin. To this he nodded assent and little by little drew near the side of our vessel, thinking he would have the axe. But one of our men, who was in our dinghy, caught hold of his canoe, and at once two or three more stepped down into it and made the Indians come on board our vessel, at which they were greatly astonished. When they had come on board, they were assured by the captain that no harm would befall them, while at the same time every sign of affection was shown to them; and they were made to eat and to drink and to be of good cheer. And then we explained to them by signs that the cross had been set up to serve as a land-mark and guide-post on coming into the harbour, and that we would soon come back and would bring them iron wares and other goods; and that we wished to take two of his [the chief's] sons away with us and afterwards would bring them back again to that harbour. And we dressed up his two sons in shirts and ribbons and in red caps, and put a little brass chain around the neck of each, at which they were greatly pleased; and they proceeded to hand over their old rags to those who were going back on shore. To each of these three, whom we sent back, we also gave a hatchet and two knives . . . .

*   *   *

And afterwards, that is to say on [Saturday] August 15, . . . we set forth . . . after hearing mass . . . and we reached the harbour of St. Malo whence we had set forth, on [Saturday] September 5 in the said year [1534].

3. "A CHAPTER ON SOME INFORMATION WHICH THE NATIVES GAVE US AFTER OUR RETURN FROM HOCHELAGA, 1535-1536" (Biggar, *The Voyages of Jacques Cartier*, pp. 200-201).

. . . And we learned from Chief Donnacona . . . and others that . . . the "river of the Saguenay" reaches to the [Kingdom of the] Saguenay. . . . And they gave us to understand, that in that country the natives go clothed and dressed in woollens like ourselves; that there are many towns and tribes composed of honest folk who possess great store of gold and copper.

*4. "LIST OF MEN AND EFFECTS FOR CANADA, SEPTEMBER 1538" (Biggar, *A Collection of Documents Relating to Jacques Cartier and the Sieur de Roberval*, pp. 70-72).

We see by this memorandum the piety, magnaminity, and generosity of heart of the great King Francis who, notwithstanding that wars had depleted his treasury and even produced immense debts, took advantage of the peaceful times, and without fear, further indebted himself to establish the Christian religion in the country of the Indians far from France . . . where he knew full well that there was no gold or silver mines, nor any other wealth but the conquest of an infinite number of souls for God and their deliverance from the dominion and tyranny of the infernal Demon to whom they, till that time, sacrificed their children.

. . . To make the trip to Canada commanded by our Sovereign Lord . . . the following numbers of ships and people are required . . . :

item: 120 mariners . . .
item: 40 musketers . . .
item: 30 carpenters . . .
item: 10 master masons . . .
item: 4 blacksmiths to search for, and explore, iron mines . . .
item: 2 goldsmiths and silversmiths who are also jewel makers . . .
item: 6 priests . . . .

FRANÇOIS

5. "LETTER OF LAGARDO* TO JOHN THE THIRD, KING OF PORTUGAL, JANUARY 22, 1539 (?) "
(Biggar, *A Collection of Documents Relating to Jacques Cartier and the Sieur de Roberval*, pp. 75-78).

. . . And the following night the King again examined the charts, and conversed more than an hour with me, . . . and he showed me a river in the land of Cod . . . and he has dispatched thither a Breton pilot named Jacques Cartier, who lives in Brittany, in a town called St. Malo; and in the two voyages he made . . . on the first he lost two ships . . . , and on the second one . . . ; and on the last voyage he brought back three Indians, two of whom are dead, the one who is left being king of three or four towns. . . . And thus he told me that the river he sent to discover . . . is eight hundred leagues long, and well up the river are two falls . . . ; and beyond the falls the King of France says the Indian King told him there is a large city called Sagana, where there are many mines of gold and silver in great abundance, and men who dress and wear shoes like we do; and that there is abundance of cloves, nutmeg, and pepper. And thus I believe he will again decide to send there a third time seeing his great desire; and thus he told me that he wished to build a fort well up the river, on the north side, and that commencing it in the summer, in the following year the brigantines may go there to pass the falls, . . . and that

---
* A Spanish spy.

there are certain animals whose hides as leather are worth ten cruzadoes
each. . . . And . . . Jacques Cartier brought to the King a sample of gold
. . . and he says it is fine gold and comes from the said city of Sagana.

*6. "CARTIER'S COMMISSION FOR HIS THIRD VOYAGE, OCTOBER 17,
     1540" (Biggar, *A Collection of Documents Relating to
     Jacques Cartier and the Sieur de Robetrval*, pp. 128-29).

. . . From those counties we have brought back several men and have
kept them in our kingdom so as to instruct them in the love and fear of
God, his holy and Christian doctrine so as to be better able, when they
return with a large number of our subjects, to induce their brethren to
accept our holy faith; and, as well, in the past, we have sent Jacques
Cartier, who discovered the great lands of Canada and Hochelaga which
are an extremity of Eastern Asia, in which, as he has reported, there is
much wealth. . . . We have decided to again send Cartier to Canada and
Hochelaga, and as far as the lands of Saguenay . . . with a goodly number
of ships and men of all rank, skills, and trades . . . so that we may better
fulfil our intention and to do actions agreeable to God our creator and
redeemer.

THE KING [FRANÇOIS]

*7. "ROBERVAL'S COMMISSION, JANUARY 15, 1541"
     (Biggar, *A Collection of Documents Relating to Jacques
     Cartier and the Sieur de Roberval*, pp. 178-85).

. . . It is our intention . . . to return to . . . Canada and Hochelaga . . .
and adjacent areas, inhabited or otherwise, but not under the sovereignty
of any other Christian Prince . . . with a large number of our citizens of
all estates and trades . . . to inhabit the lands and countries, and to construct cities, forts, and churches . . . .
. . . In order to encourage . . . those who will undertake the expedition
. . . we grant to our Lieutenant full power and authority in the lands . . .
to grant in fief and seigniory . . . and, if our Lieutenant thinks it advisable, he may remit for six years . . . any incomes due to us. . . . In addition,
. . . to those who have made the voyage . . . will be given ⅓ of the profits
. . . and a like amount to our Lieutenant . . . the remaining third is
reserved to our use . . . .

THE KING

8. "REPORT AND MEMORIAL OF THE COUNCIL OF THE INDIES*
UPON MATTERS RELATING TO THE FLEET, BEFORE MARCH 24,
1541" (Biggar, *A Collection of Documents Relating to
Jacques Cartier and the Sieur de Roberval*, pp. 244-46).

The Council of the Indies have considered the sections of the letter
addressed by your Majesty . . . concerning the French pirates alleged to
have set out from France. . . .
And as to the rumour that the intention is to form settlements in the
Northern Sea, there is no place to which the French could go which is
suitable or of any value. . . . Therefore pirates who set out for adventure
have clearly no intention of seizing lands but rather of seizing gold
and silver coming from the Indies—this is their booty. . . .

JUAN DE SAMANCO

9. "HARO TO THE EMPEROR, APRIL 5, 1541" (Biggar, *A Collection of Documents Relating to Jacques Cartier and the
Sieur de Roberval*, pp. 259-61).

Sacred Imperial Catholic Majesty [Charles V]:
Pedro de Santiago, the person who went to France, returned . . . and
brings report of the mission he was charged with, that is, to obtain information. . . . He . . . says that by order of the King of France thirteen ships
are being fitted . . . well equipped with artillery and all kinds of arms
and ammunition, and a good supply of provisions, for more than two
years, so it is said; the command of the fleet being committed to one
Jacques Cartier. . . .
And the said . . . Santiago . . . spoke to Jacques Cartier . . . and asked
the purpose of all these supplies, . . . they were destined for a country
called Canada, where they were to form a settlement and build a fort,
and they carried stone-cutters and carpenters, and smiths and all sorts of
workmen with iron tools. . . .

CHRISTOVAL DE HARO

10. "EXAMINATION OF NEWFOUNDLAND SAILORS REGARDING
CARTIER, 23 SEPTEMBER, 1542" (Biggar, *A Collection of
Documents Relating to Jacques Cartier and the Sieur
de Roberval*, pp. 449-52).

---

* The Spanish equivalent of the French Ministère de la Marine. Samanco was
president of the Council.

The said Robert Lefand. . . . asked whether he saw Jacques Cartier
or Roberval . . . , said that this witness heard . . . that Cartier left Honfleur over a year ago with three ships bound for Terra Nova. . . . The
said Jacques Cartier came . . . and he had eleven barrels of gold ore and
close on a fanega of precious stones, rubies and diamonds.

                                                              ANTONIA DE UBILLA

B

L'ENRACINEMENT

The roots of Canadian society during the French Régime were
planted, and nurtured, by Champlain. Canada, after the repeated failures and shattered hopes of the sixteenth century, had a "bad press".
"False as a diamond of Canada" was a current saying. The French State
and business community were loath to pour good money after bad.
Champlain, a mariner, explorer, geographer, author, propagandist, fur
trader, soldier, colonist, and governor, by incessant effort kindled, and
kept alive, the ever-wavering French interest in Canada.

Prior French endeavours in North America are summarized in Documents 11 and 12. In the remaining selections on this theme, 13 to 17, we
see that Champlain directed a three-pronged attack to interest the
French State, business men, and clergy in Canada. Glory and profit were
promised: a great kingdom, fabulous wealth, and a lush harvest of souls
were to be had in Canada, according to Champlain. His dreams, however, were balanced by a practical approach to the problems of colonization. The political, economic, military, and religious requirements
of a new-born colony were carefully catalogued. Today, the record of
his efforts in Canada is called history; in his own times it was an invalu-
able manual on colonization.

11. "BIARD'S RELATION OF 1616, ON THE LOCATION OF NEW
    FRANCE, AND THOSE WHO FIRST ATTEMPTED TO SETTLE
    THERE" (Thwaites, *Jesuit Relations*, Vol. 3, pp. 39-45).

We call New France, the lands and countries of America or the West Indies, which are upon the other shore of the Ocean Guienne, towards the setting sun, opposite us and lying directly in the same line from East to West. They have given it this name of New France [because] . . . this country was first discovered by French Bretons, in the year 1504, one hundred and eleven years ago, and since then they have not ceased to visit it. The Normans also assisted in these early discoveries; among whom we read that Captain Thomas Aubert, of Dieppe, sailed in the year 1508, and brought back from there some Natives, whom he exhibited to the wonder and applause of France. Two years before him, Captain Jean Denys, of Honfleur, had made the same discovery; but, as he brought back only some fish, and Geographical charts, he has not become so renowned as Thomas Aubert. After the year 1523, Jean Verazan skirted all the coast of Florida to Cape Breton, and took possession of it in the name of his master, Francis I. I believe it was Jean Verazan who was godfather to this title of "New France" for Canada (a name by which they also frequently call it) is not, properly speaking, all this extent of country which they now call New France; but it is only that part, which extends along the banks of the great River Canada, and the Gulf of St. Lawrence; this being only the most Northern part of New France. . . .

Now ever since the first of these discoveries, the French have been talking about cultivating and inhabiting these wildernesses. . . . Certain individuals, such as Roberval and the Marquis de la Roche and others, have even attempted it. But the most widely known and latest voyage undertaken for this purpose was that of Sieur de Monts, Pierre de Gua, who has been very highly commended for it. Having considerable money at his disposal, and having associated with him for this object certain Merchants of Rouen, of St. Malo and of la Rochelle, he received from the late Henry the Great, . . . full power and authority, as Lieutenant of the King in these countries, from the fortieth to the forty-sixth parallel of latitude, for there ended the power given him to dispose of lands.

Now Sieur de Monts, having the authority and power mentioned, and being well equipped and accompanied, left France in the year 1604, just a hundred years after the discovery of this country, and went to live upon the Coast of Norembegue among the Eteminquoys people, upon a small Island, which he called Sainte Croix. But misfortune overtook him there, for he lost a great many people by sickness.

Leaving there the following year, forced by necessity, he changed his dwelling place to Port Royal, towards the east-south-east, . . . in Acadie . . . . Here he remained only two years, for the associated merchants, seeing that their outlay exceeded their receipts, no longer cared to continue the experiment. . . . These are all the chief results of our efforts up to the years 1610 and 1611. . . .

12. "CHAMPLAIN'S SUMMARY"
(Biggar, *The Works of Samuel de Champlain*, Vol. 1,
pp. 229-32).

After them, notwithstanding all these vicissitudes and hesitations, the
Sieur de Monts desired to attempt this desperate undertaking, and asked
His Majesty for a commission for this purpose; for he realized that what
had ruined the former undertakings had been a lack of assistance to the
promoters, who, neither in a single year nor in two, had been able to
become acquainted with the regions and the peoples who inhabit them,
or to find harbours suitable for settlement. He proposed to His Majesty
a method of meeting expenses without drawing anything from the royal
exchequer, namely, that he be given a monopoly of the fur trade of that
country. This having been granted to him, he contracted large and
excessive expenditure, and took with him a considerable number of
men of divers conditions, and had constructed there the dwellings necessary for his men. This expenditure he continued for three consecutive
years, after which, in consequence of the jealousy, and importunity of
certain Basque and Breton merchants, his grant was revoked by the
Council, to the great detriment of the said Sieur de Monts, who, in consequence of this revocation, was compelled to abandon everything, with
the loss of his labour and all his implements wherewith he had provided
the settlement.

But as he had made a report to the king of the fertility of the soil, and
I had made one upon the means of discovering the passage to China without the inconvenience of the northern icebergs, or the heat of the torrid
zone through which our seamen, with incredible labours and perils, pass
twice in going and twice in returning, his Majesty commanded the Sieur
de Monts to prepare a fresh expedition and again to send men to continue what he had begun. This he did; and because of the uncertainty
of his commission he changed the locality to deprive his rivals of the
distrust he had aroused in them. He was influenced also by the hope of
greater advantages in the interior, where the people are civilised, and
where it is easier to plant the Christian faith and to establish such order
as is necessary for the preservation of a country than along the sea-
shore where the Indians usually dwell . . . .

13. "ON THE UTILITY OF COMMERCE, 1613" (Biggar, *The
Works of Samuel de Champlain*, Vol. 1, pp. 225-32).

According to the diversity of their dispositions, man's inclinations
vary, and each in his calling has a particular object. Some aim at profit,
others at glory, and others at the public welfare. The greater number take

to commerce, and especially that which is carried on by sea. Thence springs the people's principal source of comfort, with the wealth and honour of states. This it was that raised ancient Rome to the sovereignty and mastery of the whole world, and the Venetians to a height comparable with that of mighty kings. In all ages it has made maritime nations abound in riches, among which cities Alexandria and Tyre are so famous, and a host of others occupying the interiors of the countries, while foreign nations have sent them whatever beautiful and remarkable things they possess. This is why many princes have striven to find a route to China by the north, in order to facilitate commerce with the peoples of the East, in the hope that this route might prove shorter and less dangerous.

* * *

So many voyages and explorations at the cost of so much effort and expense having been undertaken in vain, our Frenchmen were induced in these last few years to endeavour to effect a permanent settlement in those lands which we call New France, in the hope of attaining more easily to the completion of this enterprise. . . .

14. "BIARD'S RELATION, 1616"
(Thwaites, *Jesuit Relations*, Vol. 3, p. 161).

. . . You have been told how, towards the end of the year 1607, Sieur de Monts's entire company returned to France, and this new France was then entirely deserted by our countrymen. However, in the following year, 1608, Sieur de Monts chose as his Lieutenant Sieur de Champlain, and sent him on a tour of discovery along the great St. Lawrence river; Champlain did admirably there, establishing the settlement of Kebec . . . .

15. "WHAT LED ME TO SEEK FOR REGULATIONS . . . , 1613"
(Biggar, *The Works of Samuel de Champlain*, Vol. 2, pp. 241-44).

The desire I have always entertained of making new discoveries in New France for the welfare, advantage, and the glory of the French name, as well as of bringing these poor peoples to the knowledge of God, has led me more and more to try to find facilities for this undertaking, which can be brought about only by proper regulations. So long as everyone wishes to gather the fruits of my labour without contributing to the cost and to the large outlay necessary for the maintenance of the settlements which are required in order to bring these projects to a successful end, will this trade be ruined through the greed of gain, which is so great that it prompts merchants to set sail before the proper season, and to rush not only into the ice, but also to their own ruin, in order to arrive first in this country. For, when they trade secretly with the natives, and, vying with one another, give more merchandise than is necessary, they buy the Indians' commodities too dearly, and so, whilst to deceive their associates, more often deceive themselves.

* * *

And knowing that Monseigneur the Count de Soissons was a devout prince and kindly disposed towards all godly enterprises, I approached him . . . and pointed out to him the importance of the matter, and showed him the way to regulate it. . . . When he was informed of all the details of the matter . . . he promised me, subject to the king's good pleasure, to take the enterprise under his patronage.
. . . His Majesty gave the direction and control . . . to the . . . Count, who immediately honoured me by appointing me his Lieutenant.

16. "TO THE KING AND THE LORDS OF HIS COUNCIL,
[BEFORE] 1618" (Biggar, *The Works of Samuel de Champlain*, Vol. 2, pp. 326-28).

The Sieur de Champlain represents to you most humbly that for sixteen years he has toiled with laborious zeal as well in the discoveries of New France as of divers peoples and nations whom he has brought to our knowledge, . . . which peoples have given him such and so faithful report of the north and south seas that one cannot doubt but that this would be the means of reaching easily to the Kingdom of China and the East Indies, whence great riches could be drawn; besides planting there the divine worship, as our Recollet friars can bear witness, in addition to the abundance of merchandise from the said country of New France, which would be drawn thence annually through the diligence of the workmen who would go there. Should this said country be given up and the settlement abandoned, . . . the English or Flemings, envious of our prosperity, would seize upon it, thereby enjoying the fruits of our labours, and preventing by this means more than a thousand vessels from going to the dry and green fisheries and for whale-oil. . . .

17. "STATEMENT OF PERSONS TO BE BROUGHT AND MAINTAINED
AT THE QUEBEC SETTLEMENT FOR THE YEAR 1619"
(Biggar, *The Works of Samuel de Champlain*, Vol. 4, pp. 353-54).

There will be 80 persons, including the leader, three Recollet Fathers, clerks, officers, craftsmen, and field labourers.

For every two persons there will be a mattress, a straw bed, two blankets, three pairs of new sheets, two coats apiece, six shirts, four pairs of shoes, and a cloak.

For arms, 40 muskets with their shoulder belts, 24 pikes, 4 wheel-locks four to five feet long, 1000 lbs. of fine powder, 1000 lbs. of cannon-powder, 1000 lbs. of balls for the cannon, six thousand-weight of lead, a puncheon of cannon match.

For the men, a dozen scythes with handles, hammers, and other tools, 12 sickles, 24 spades for turning up the soil, 12 pickaxes, 4000 lbs. of iron, 2 barrels of steel, 10 tons of lime . . . , ten thousand curved tiles or twenty thousand flat, ten thousand bricks for making an oven and chimneys, two mill-stones, . . .

For the service of the leader's table, 36 platters, as many bowls and plates, 6 salt-cellars, 6 ewers, 2 basins, 6 jugs holding 2 pints each, 6 pint-pots, 6 half-pints, 6 quarter-pints, all of tin, two dozen table-cloths, 24 dozen napkins.

For the kitchen, a dozen copper cauldrons, 6 pairs of andirons, 6 frying-pans, 6 gridirons.

There will also be brought two yearling bulls, heifers, and sheep; as much as possible of all kinds of grain for sowing.

C

THE JESUITS, THE FRENCH STATE

AND NEW FRANCE

The Jesuits came to Quebec in 1625. The members of the Society of Jesus (their official name) were religious activists. The order was organized along military lines. Their colleges, clerical West Points, submitted novices to a long and intense training and education before permitting them to take their place in the secular world as missionaries, scientists, educators, philosophers, advisers, and confessors to rulers, in Europe, Asia, Africa, and America.

Jesuit interest in New France is significant not merely because it produced martyrs for the faith but because the Society had wealth and power, two indispensable requirements for successful colonial endeavours. It had access to the purse of the wealthy and the minds of the powerful.

The Order's soldiers submitted annual reports to the General of the Society. These were published, often annually, as *The Jesuit Relations*. Many of the documents to follow are drawn from this rich and varied collection of historical data.

A more direct participation of the French State in the colonization of New France is evident in Document 20. The state-organized and -subsidized Company of New France, or of the 100 Associates, formed in 1627, was primarily the handiwork of Richelieu, chief minister to the King, Louis XIII. By it, the power and the purse of France were committed to Canada.

Before the benefits of the "new order" could be realized, disaster struck. Quebec was captured. However, France and England had ended hostilities before the fall of Quebec and the peace treaty returned the little settlement to France.

The last document, 22, is in the nature of a summary of early French interest in New France by Father DuCreux, a Jesuit, who published a History of Canada in 1664.

18. "LETTER FROM THE REVEREND FATHER CHARLES LALLEMANT,
      SUPERIOR OF THE MISSIONS IN CANADA, TO SIEUR DE CHAM-
      PLAIN, KEBEC, THIS 28TH DAY OF JULY, 1625"
      (Thwaites, *Jesuit Relations*, Vol. 4, p. 171).

Thanks to God, here we are in the district of your Lieutenancy, where we arrived after having one of the most successful voyages ever yet experienced. Monsieur the General, after having told us that is was impossible to give us lodging either in the settlement or in the fort, and that we must either return to France, or withdraw to the Recollet Fathers' obliged us to accept the latter offer. The Fathers received us with so much charity, that we feel forever under obligation to them. Our Lord will be their reward. One of our Fathers, together with the Recollet Father who came from France, went to the trading station with the intention of going to the Hurons or to the Hiroquois, as they should think best after consulting Father Nicolas, who was to be at this station to confer with them. But it happened that poor Father Nicolas was drowned in the last of the rapids, for which reason they returned, as they knew no one there, and had no knowledge of the language or of the country. We are therefore awaiting your arrival to determine what it will be well to do . . . .

19. "CHARLES L'ALLEMANT, SUPERIOR OF THE MISSION OF CANADA, TO FATHER JEROME L'ALLEMANT, HIS BROTHER, QUEBEC, AUGUST 1, 1626" (Thwaites, *Jesuit Relations,* Vol. 4, pp. 197-201, 207-9).

*   *   *

As to the customs of the Savages, it is enough to say that they are altogether savage. From morning until night they have no other thought than to fill their stomachs. They come to see us only to ask for something to eat; and if you do not give it to them they show their dissatisfaction. They are real beggars, if there ever were any, and yet as proud as they can be. They consider the French less intelligent than they. Vices of the flesh are very common among them. One of them will marry several women, and will leave them when he pleases, and take others. There is one here who married his own daughter, but all the other Savages were indignant at him for it. As to cleanliness among them, that never enters into the question; they are very dirty about their eating, and in their cabins they are covered with vermin, which they eat when they catch them. It is a custom of this Tribe to kill their fathers and mothers when they are so old that they can walk no longer, thinking that they are thus doing them a good service; for otherwise, they would be compelled to die of hunger, as they have become unable to follow the others when they change their location. When I had it explained to one of them one day that the same thing would be done for him when he became old, he answered that he certainly expected it. Their method of making war against their enemies is generally through treachery, watching to find them alone; and, if they are not strong enough to make prisoners of those whom they encounter, they shoot them with their arrows, then cut off their heads, which they bring back to show their people. But, if they can take them to their cabins as prisoners, they subject them to unparalleled cruelties, killing them by inches; and, strange to say, during all these tortures, the victims sing constantly, considering it a dishonour if he cries out or complains. After the victim is dead, they eat him, and no one is so insignificant that he does not get his share. . . . At the feast which are given in honour of the death of someone, they set aside a part for the deceased as well as for the others. . . . They bury the dead, and with them all their belongings, such as candlesticks, furs, knives, etc. . . . Thus they believe . . . in the immortality of our souls; and, in fact, they assure you that after death they go to Heaven, where they eat mushrooms and hold intercourse with each other.

All of their wealth consists in the furs of different animals, but principally of the Beaver. Before the time of the association of those Gentlemen to whom the King gave this trade for a certain time in consideration of certain conditions mentioned in the Articles, the Savages were visited by many people, to such an extent that an Old Man told me he had seen as many as twenty ships in the port of Tadoussac. But now since this business has been granted to the association, which to-day has a monopoly over all others, we see here not more than two ships which belong to it, and that only once a year, about the beginning of the month of June. These two ships bring all the merchandise which these Gentlemen use in trading with the Savages; that is to say, the cloaks, blankets, nightcaps, hats, shirts, sheets, hatchets, iron arrowheads, bodkins, swords, picks to break the ice in Winter, knives, kettles, prunes, raisins, Indian corn, peas, cracker or sea biscuits, and tobacco; and what is necessary for the sustenance of the French in this country besides. In exchange for these they carry back hides of the moose, linx, fox, otter, black ones being encountered occasionally, martens, badgers, and muskrats; but they deal principally in Beavers, in which they find their greatest profit. I was told that during one year they carried back as many as 22,000. The usual number for one year is 15,000 or 12,000, at one pistole each, which is not doing badly. It is true their expenses are very heavy, as they keep here forty persons and more, who are paid and maintained; this is in addition to the expense of the crews of the two ships, which consist of at least 150 men, who receive their wages and food. These wages are not all the same. They are generally 106 livres, but some receive a hundred écus. I know an interpreter who receives one hundred pistoles, and a certain number of hides which he is permitted to carry away each year . . . .

*20. "ESTABLISHMENT OF THE COMPANY OF THE 100 ASSOCIATES,
APRIL 29, 1627" (*Édits et Ordonnances*, pp. 5-11).

. . . Those to whom we had entrusted the care of the colony were so little interested that, to date, there is but one settlement . . . in which are maintained forty or fifty Frenchmen favouring the interests of the merchants rather than the . . . interests of the King; so badly maintained have they been . . . and so neglected has been the development of agriculture that if yearly provisions had been delayed . . . the small group of inhabitants would have starved to death, having but one month's supplies in store . . . .

The disorders have reached such a point that . . . to assist in the conversion of the indigenous inhabitants and to establish a prosperous colony . . . New France should be, once and for all, made part of the King's domain . . . .

1— . . . The Hundred Associates promise to transport two or three hundred settlers of all trades by 1628 and in the following fifteen years, until a total of four thousand is reached . . . and to shelter, nourish and maintain them . . . for three years . . . .

2— . . . It will not be permitted, however, to transport aliens . . . but rather the colony must be settled by French Catholic citizens . . . .

3— In each settlement established by the Associates there are to be at least three clerics in order to . . . convert the Indians and bring spiritual comfort to the French citizens. . . . The Associates will furnish . . . all the requirements necessary to the fulfilment of the spiritual functions for fifteen years; however, should the Associates so choose, they may distribute to the clerics cleared lands sufficient for their maintenance . . . .

4— . . . His Majesty will grant, in perpetuity, to the . . . One Hundred Associates . . . plenary property, justice, and seigniorial rights . . . to Quebec . . . all of New France . . . from the coast of Florida . . . to the Artic circle . . . and from the Island of Newfoundland . . . west to the great lake . . . .

7— Further, His Majesty grants . . . forever all traffic in pelts and furs . . . ; and for fifteen years . . . all other commerce . . . except . . . cod fishing and whaling which His Majesty wishes to be free to all his subjects . . . .

8— . . . French inhabitants and their families settled in the country and not maintained by the . . . Company . . . may engage in the fur trade . . . as long as the pelts are sold to the Company . . . .

9— In addition, His Majesty will give to the Associates two warships . . . armed and equipped . . . .

13— And to further encourage His Majesty's subjects to immigrate, and produce manufactured goods, His Majesty will grant to all artisans . . . who practise their trade in New France . . . a master's certificate after six years . . . .

14— . . . All merchandise . . . manufactured in New France . . . will be exempted from all import duties . . . for fifteen years . . . .

15— . . . All necessary supplies for New France will be exempted from . . . all duties . . . .

17— . . . The descendants of Frenchmen, as well as any converted natives . . . will be considered . . . as . . . French citizens and as such may live in France . . . without any further declaration of naturalization . . . .

ARMAND, CARDINAL DE RICHELIEU ETC.

21. "THE CAPTURE OF QUEBEC, 1629" (Biggar, *The Works of Samuel de Champlain*, Vol. 6, pp. 52-55).

. . . It was decided that, considering our helpless situation in being without provisions, powder or match, and destitute of help, it was impossible to hold out, and that we must therefore seek the most advantageous terms of capitulation possible . . . .

When the tide came in, the English sent a boat with a white flag as a signal to inquire if they might safely come and summon us and learn what was our determination. I hoisted another flag on the fort to let them know that they might approach in all security. When they had arrived at our settlement, an English gentleman set foot on shore, and came to see me, courteously handing me a letter from the two brothers of General Kirke who was at Tadoussac with his vessels. One, called Captain Louis, came to take command at the fort, and the other, Captain Thomas, Vice-Admiral of his brother; and this was what they write to me:

> Sir, In pursuance of what my brother wrote to you last year, that sooner or later he would take possession of Quebec, unless it were reinforced, he has instructed us to assure you of his friendship, as we assure you of ours, and knowing well the state of extreme destitution in which you are with respect to everything, he calls upon you to place the fort and habitation in our hands. . . . Your very affectionate servants, Louis and Thomas Kirke. On board the Flyboat, this nineteenth of July, 1629.

This letter having been read . . . it was decided to reply to the letter as follows:

> Gentlemen, The truth is that negligence, or the hindrances caused by the bad weather, or the perils of the sea have prevented the arrival of the relief that we were expecting in our suffering, and have put it out of our power to resist the carrying out of your design. . . . Champlain. This nineteenth of July, 1629.

22. "THE HISTORY OF CANADA OR NEW FRANCE BY FATHER FRANÇOIS DU CREU, S.J." (Du Creux, *The History of Canada or New France*, pp. 18, 27, 28, 37, 134, 204).

EARLY SETTLEMENTS

In the end of the last century the following explorers turned their steps in the direction of North America, Jacques Cartier and Jean Francois de la Roque, Sieur de Roberval. In the beginning of the present century the Marquis de la Roche, Sieur de Monts and Pontgravé followed their example, and, though these adventurers accomplished little beyond a careful exploration of the coasts, their efforts inspired Samuel de Champlain to make a friendly alliance with the natives, in order to secure if possible, the fur trade. Nor would Champlain's efforts have been successful had not God promoted the high designs of Father Pierre Coton, and had not the Marquise de Guercheville, a lady of tried virtue, been finally induced by the exhortations of the same Coton to undertake this noble task and to form a company for this very purpose with the consent of Henry the Great; this company included certain Calvinists, for there were none among the orthodox with whom he could bargain;

the object of this company was to send certain workers from the Society
of Jesus to work both difficult and pleasing to God.

ON THE PURCHASE OF THE MONOPOLY
OF CANADA

. . . the best thing to do would be for the Duke to purchase the
office of Viceroy of New France from his uncle the Duc de Montmorency.
. . . Montmorency, who then held the office, was by nature more fitted
for arms than for settling the disputes of traders, and that he was weary
of the troublesome business and he would not be reluctant to relinquish
both the burden and the dignity upon honourable terms. Without delay
Ventadour conferred with Montmorency, and agreed to pay something
over a hundred thousand livre; . . .

ON RICHELIEU

And such was the power of Richelieu at this time that he was at once
able to gather together from the whole of France a company of about a
hundred men of wealth and affluence, who were not only Catholics but
eminent in their piety, who made an honourable covenant with the King,
by which they were to hold all Canada with sovereign rights and to
divide among themselves the profits of the trade with New France.

ON THE RESTITUTION OF NEW FRANCE

The matter was now settled and at the beginning of 1632 the question
of the appointment of a new governor to resume possession of New
France began to be discussed. Samuel de Champlain seemed to be the
most suitable person; he had the necessary experience, he was zealous
in propagating the faith, and in addition he was acceptable to both the
French and the natives; . . . but time did not permit the raising of money
or the securing of ships, and so for the present it seemed best to appoint
William de Caen who was a man of means and, though a Calvinist,
moderate in his opinions. There was the additional reason that, since the
English had inflicted a heavy loss upon de Caen three years before, it
seemed fair to compensate him by this new commission.

ON CHAMPLAIN

He bore the whole burden of administration on his own shoulders,
giving armed assistance to those of the savages who seemed in any way
eager for the friendship of the French, as well as those who did not
reject it when offered; explored new territory; chose with wisdom the
site of a new post; was active for the public or private advantage of the
French and the savages; . . .

PART II

1635-1663

The thousands of words written on the martyrdom of the Jesuits in this era in which they played a dominant role have resulted in an under-estimation of the Jesuits' other contributions to the formation of the society of New France. The work of the Jesuits, however spiritual its end, could only be fulfilled through a material foundation. These churchmen were funnels of French culture: for this reason Documents 23 and 24 present the Jesuits as secular agents.

The blend of spiritual and material is nowhere better seen than in the establishment of Montreal. It was originally founded as a centre for the conversion of the Indians, but rapidly became the dominant centre of the fur trade. Themes B and C consider both the original purpose and the ultimate importance of Montreal. In both, the Indians play a central role: they are the souls to be saved and are also the means to the fur trade. To the Iroquois, Montreal was more than a mystic realization; it was a very direct threat to their commercial empire. And when the Iroquois massacred the early settlers of Montreal, the Jesuits in the hinterland, and the allies of the French, the Hurons, they were not merely killing Catholics, but more important, Frenchmen or friends of Frenchmen. Both were economic rivals.

Despite the violence and insecurity of the era, Canadian society developed. A new class, a secular aristocracy, arose. In time, it would replace the Church as the dominant element in the colony. This group of Frenchmen made Canada their homeland. Trade was, at first, their principal occupation. They soon demanded, and were granted, political recognition. This development is presented in theme D.

The intense economic activity of the new class, and constant geo-spiritual expansion of the Jesuits, brought about a crisis in foreign relations. As the conflict deepened, greater aid was required to survive. Towards the end of the period the arrival of Laval as head of the Canadian Church, and the inquiry of the King's investigator Gaudais, presaged Royal Government. These events are illustrated in themes E, F, and G.

A

THE JESUITS AS SECULAR AGENTS

Champlain's mantle as the protector, propagandist, and colonial agent of New France fell upon the Jesuits after his death in 1635. Documents 23 and 24 repeat some of Champlain's injunctions and appeals, and add new ones as well. The secular role of the Jesuits was all the more significant when one remembers that the fall of Quebec in 1629 had seriously depleted the capital of the Company of New France.

23. "LEJEUNE'S RELATION OF 1635"
(Thwaites, *Jesuit Relations*, Vol. 8, pp. 9-13).

It is to be feared that in the multiplication of our French in these countries, peace, happiness, and good feeling may not increase in the same ratio as do the Inhabitants of New France. It is much easier to control a few men than a multitude; yet it must be confessed that it would be an enterprise very honorable and very profitable to Old France, and very useful to the New, to establish settlements here, and to send over Colonists.

Shall the French, alone of all the Nations of the earth, be deprived of the honor of expanding and spreading over this New World? Shall France much more populous than all the other Kingdoms, have inhabi-

tants only for itself? or, when her children leave her, shall they go here
and there and lose the name Frenchmen among Foreigners?

*   *   *

... Would it not be better to empty Old France into New, by means
of Colonies which could be sent there, than to people Foreign countries?

Add to this, if you please, that there is a multitude of workmen in
France, who, for lack of employment or of owning a little land, pass their
lives in poverty and wretched want. Many of them beg their bread from
door to door; some of them resort to stealing and public brigandage,
others to larceny and secret frauds, each one trying to obtain for himself
what many cannot possess. Now as New France is so immense, so many
inhabitants can be sent here that those who remain in the Mother Country will have enough honest work left them to do, without launching into
those vices which ruin Republics; this does not mean that ruined people,
or those of evil lives, should be sent here, for that would be to build
Babylons; but if the good were to make room for the bad, it would give
the latter an opportunity to escape the idleness that corrupts them.

Besides, if these Countries are peopled by our French, not only will
this weaken the strength of the Foreigner,—who holds in his ships, in his
towns, and in his armies, a great many of our Countrymen as hostages,
—not only will it banish famine from the houses of the multitude of poor
workmen, but it will also strengthen France; for those who will be born
in New France, will be French, and in the case of need can render good
service to their King,—a thing which cannot be expected from those who
dwell among our neighbours and outside the dominion of their Prince.

Finally, if this country is peopled by the French, it will be firmly
attached to the Crown, and the Foreigner will come no more to trouble
it . . . .

Now, there is no doubt that there can be found here employment for
all sorts of artisans. Why cannot the great forests of New France largely
furnish the ships for the Old? Who doubts that there are here mines of
iron, copper, and other metals? Some have already been discovered,
which will soon be worked; and hence all those who work in wood and
iron will find employment here. Grain will not fail here, more than in
France. . . . I will content myself by saying that it would be an honor
and a great benefit to both Old and New France to send over Emigrants
and establish strong colonies in these lands, . . .

24. "SOME ADVICE TO THOSE WHO DESIRE TO CROSS OVER INTO
     NEW FRANCE, LEJEUNE'S RELATION, 1636"
     (Thwaites, *Jesuit Relations*, Vol. 9, pp. 185-91).

All those who desire to come and increase this Colony are either people of means, or poor people; I will speak to both. Let us begin with the poor.

A poor man burdened with a wife and children should not come over here the first years with his family, if he is not hired by the Gentlemen of the Company, or by someone else who will bring them hither; otherwise he will suffer greatly, and will not make any headway. The Country is not yet in a condition to care for the poor who cannot work. But if there happens to be some worthy young men or able-bodied married men, who can handle the axe, the hoe, the spade, and the plough — such people, if willing to work, could become rich in a little while in this Country, to which they could finally bring their families. This is the way they should proceed.

Four or five of them would have to join together, and engage themselves to some family for five or six years on the following conditions: That they should be boarded during all this time without receiving any wages, but also that they should possess entirely and in their own right one-half of all the land they clear. And, as they will need something for their own support, the contract should provide that all they get every year, from the lands they have already cleared, should be shared by half; this half, with the little profits they can make in the Country, would be enough to keep them, and to pay after the first or second year for half the tools which they will use in clearing and tilling the land. Now if four men could clear eight arpents of land a year, doing nothing else, winter and summer, in six years forty-eight arpents would be cleared, of which twenty-four would belong to them. With these twenty-four arpents they could support thirty-six persons, or even forty-eight, if the land is good. Is this not the way of becoming rich in a little while? And, all the more so, as the lands here will one day become profitable and will bear a great deal of grain. There is now brought here from France so much flour, . . . that if someone planted wheat here . . . he would derive much profit therefrom. There are so many strong and robust peasants in France who have no bread to put in their mouths; is it possible that they are so afraid of losing sight of the village steeple, as they say, that they would rather languish in their misery and poverty, than to place themselves some day at their ease among the inhabitants of New France, where with the blessings of the earth they will far more easily find those of heaven and of the soul? For debauchery, dissoluteness and intrigues are not yet current here. But to whom do I speak? To people who cannot know what I am writing, unless more capable ones than they tell it to them. These I beg to do so, in the name of God and of the King; for the interests of both are involved in peopling this country.

As to the people of wealth and rank, I would advise them before coming here to obtain from the Gentlemen of the Company a place to build a house in the town which has been laid out, and also a few arpents of land near the town, capable of sustaining their families. In addition to this, a grant of some fine locality which they will choose in the course of time. When this has been accomplished, they must bring over at least two Masons, two Carpenters, and some labourers; . . . Above all, let them have some axes made expressly, sparing no money on them, for the winter is harder than bad steel. There must be a man of authority and discretion to take care of all these people, to direct them, and to take charge of the provisions which are sent over . . . .

B

MONTREAL, A MYSTIC REALIZATION

The settlement of Ville Marie on the Island of Montreal was an act of faith, the sowing of a spiritual seed whose harvested flower was to be a bouquet of souls for God and Church. The Compagnie du Saint-Sacrement a secret society of Counter-Reformation zealots in France, was the prime mover. Le Royer de la Dauversière, the Baron de Fancamp, and Jean-Jacques Olier, who would be the founder of the Gentlemen of St. Sulpice, the eventual seigniors of the Island, founded La Société de Notre-Dame de Montreal in 1639. It was to be the agency of colonization.

The Island, however, had been previously conceded by the Company of New France. The first task was to acquire Montreal. Lauzon, the seignior, originally held the grant in another's name (Document 25). He was a prominent member of the Company of New France, and would later be a governor of the colony.

Dollier de Casson, in addition to writing a History of Montreal, laboured as a missionary and explorer, and later became Vicar-General of the Sulpicians. The practical problems of settlement and defence, as well as the motives of the *Compagnie*, are stated in his writings cited as Document 27, and in those of Olier that follow.

Marie de l'Incarnation and Marie Morin were nuns. Both left valuable records. The former, living in Quebec, kept up a voluminous correspondence. Her writings, edited in four volumes by Dom Jamet, give priceless information on the travails of the early settlers in Mont-

real. Note, by the way, the very human touch as she details the fickle-
ness of those supporting missionary endeavours.

Marie Morin was born in Montreal in 1649. She entered the order
of the Hospitalière de St. Joseph at the age of thirteen, and was an
intimate of Jeanne Mance, the founder of the Hôtel Dieu de Montréal.
Her history, written about 1697, indicates a lessening of the mystic's
concern merely for souls, and a better appreciation of the rising commercial importance of Montreal.

*25. "TRANSFER . . . OF THE CONCESSION . . . TO . . . JEAN DE
LAUZON, APRIL 30, 1638" (*Édits et Ordonnances*, pp.
245-46).

Today there appeared before [us] . . . Jacques Girard, Sieur de la
Chau . . . who admitted, confessed, and declared having no pretensions
. . . to the concession made to him on January 15, 1636 . . . in New France
of the Island of Montreal. The concession belongs to . . . Jean de Lauzon.
. . . The said Sieur de la Chaussee accepted the said concession to please,
and lend his name to, the said Sieur de Lauzon . . . .

GIRARD, HARDIN-HUART, AND HAGUENIER

*26. "CONCESSION OF A LARGE PART OF THE ISLAND OF MONTREAL
BY THE COMPANY OF ONE HUNDRED ASSOCIATES . . . ,
DECEMBER 17, 1640" (*Édits et Ordonnances*, pp. 20-23).

As our great desire is to establish a strong colony in New France so
that we may instruct the indigenous inhabitants . . . in the knowledge of
God . . . we have welcomed all those who have presented themselves to
assist us in this worthy task and have never refused them lands . . . conceded to us by the . . . King . . . for these reasons and being well informed
of the good intentions of Pierre Chevrier, esquire, Sieur de Fancamp
and of Hiérosme le Royer, Sieur de la Dauversière . . . we grant to . . .
Chevrier and le Royer . . . A large part of the island of Montreal . . . .

*27. "HISTORY OF MONTREAL" (Casson, *Histoire de Montreal*,
pp. 5-6, 31-32, 71, 82).

I send you, gentlemen, this narrative so that it may serve you as a
useful means to come to Montreal without the necessity of medications to

withstand the rigours of the voyage. If you suffer from sea-sickness do not fear the waves on this trip for the tossing of this ship will in no way augment your suffering. If you have a weak stomach, and you are apprehensive of the heartaches usually caused by an agitated sea, you may trust my word and hardily turn these pages without fear for I promise that the crossing will be so calm that you will barely notice it. If you fear the flies that we call mosquitoes that give the inhabitants so much exercise in this country, be assured that I will banish them from this book and that you will find nary a one. If the weakness of your eyes leads you to fear our snows, I offer myself as the guarantor of your sight . . . .

* * *

1640-41) . . . De Montmagny was persuaded to oppose the establishment of Montreal because of the Iroquois wars. He was told that the enterprise could never succeed . . . and that the new company was so absurd that it should be named "Absurd Enterprise", a name which the company was given among many others so that posterity might recognize that this pious folly was in the hands of God and the All Powerful, whose sagacity is sublime and beyond the understanding of the human spirit.

* * *

1648-49) . . . Summer having arrived Mlle. Mance went down to Quebec to receive the news from France which was very saddening for . . . she learned of the death of . . . Rapin, her good friend and charitable protector. . . . Secondly, that the Company of Montreal was almost dispersed, and thirdly, that de la Dauversière was almost bankrupt . . . and that . . . his goods were going to be seized . . . .

* * *

1651-52) . . . This year, the country having changed commandants, the new governor wanted to show, to the Gentlemen of Montreal, his good intentions and what might be expected . . . curtailed the 1,000 livres payment . . . given to Maisonneuve for himself as governor of Montreal, and for the garrison. I do not want to say anything detrimental about this gentleman's conduct towards the island, for I want to believe that his intentions were good, but if he had better supported this dam, the Iroquois inundations would not have so easily taken the path towards Quebec. This new governor had promised . . . ten soldiers to Maisonneuve. . . . He sent these ten soldiers to Montreal as he had promised, but he allowed them to leave so late in the year . . . and with so little clothing, that they nearly froze to death . . . .

*28. "MOTIVES FOR THE FOUNDING OF MONTREAL, ABOUT 1643"
(Olier, *Les Véritables Motifs*, pp. 1, 10, 22, 41).

First Motive: As it is the design of God to call to salvation all men, and to manifest the wisdom hidden in him for centuries, and to make known the mystery of his goodness, to all nations of the world . . . for this end he placed a church on earth . . . and honoured it as God's bride to be a mother to all the living . . . .

Second Motive: Presume this truth to be infallible: That God finds pleasing the services of those who assist in the spread of his word, and make known the merits of his blood amongst the pagan nations, and that laymen may be called, according to their means . . . .

Third Motive: This motive depends upon this truth: that meritorious spiritual endeavours, amongst which the conversion of souls is the most pleasing to God . . . are to be preferred to the temporal . . . and that the charity which has as an end the salvation of souls is as a work of pure spirituality . . . .

Fourth Motive: Not many reasons are needed to prove that among the people of America there are none so deprived of spiritual succour as those of North America wherein New France is situated . . . .

*29. "MARIE DE L'INCARNATION TO MADEMOISELLE DE LUYNES, QUEBEC, SEPTEMBER 29, 1642" (Jamet, *Marie de l'Incarnation*, Vol. 3, pp. 296-307).

. . . You know of the great affection that our good foundress, who brought us to Canada, had for us, and of her heroic generosity. She resided with us for a year continuing towards us and our seminarians these sentiments. She then began wishing to visit the Indians which is, in itself, very praiseworthy. Shortly afterwards she left us altogether, and visited us but seldom. We thought that she had an aversion to being cloistered, and as she was not a member of any order, it was reasonable to leave her free. For ourselves, we were of the opinion that as long as she helped us materially, which she solemnly promised, this departure would cause no harm to the seminary. However, time passed, and her desire to support us diminished day by day. What concerned us even more was her departure with the . . . people who arrived last year to establish a habitation at Montreal. . . . She reclaimed her furniture, and many other furnishings of the Church and the seminary, which she had given us. We let everything be taken without any repugnance, but to open my heart to you, I must avow that in returning them I felt a great joy believing that God was treating me like Saint Francis, who was abandoned by his father, and even returned the clothes he wore. It was thus with a light heart that I was despoiled leaving the seminary in dire poverty. . . . I cannot say that our good foundress errs . . . for . . . she is so pious . . . that I cannot doubt the purity of her intentions. . . . What does worry me though is her establishment at Montreal where there is an evident danger to her life because of the incursions of the Iroquois. . . . And what is even more touching is that she remains in spite of the advice of the Reverend Fathers, and M. the Governor, who have done all in their power to convince her to return . . . . These changes have put our affairs in a very bad state, for M. de Bernières . . . has told me that he can do little with the endowment we have which is only 900 livres . . . .

*30. "MARIE MORIN ON MONTREAL, 1697" (Morin, *Annales de l'Hôtel-Dieu,* pp. 24-25).

The Island of Montreal is towards the centre of Canada and is south of Quebec. . . . The circumference of the Island is said to be 30 *lieus* and there is a mountain in the middle called Mount-Royal which has given its name to the whole Island. The Island is commonly called Ville Marie . . . because M. de la Dauversière, to whom it belonged, gave it this beautiful name. He later made a gift of the island to the priests of St. Sulpice of the Seminary of Paris, who are the present seigniors and who profess a great respect and love for the Holy Virgin . . . .

Ville Marie is considered . . . the most advantageous post in New France, at least of the populated areas, for two reasons. The first is commerce, for the area is the centre to which all the Indian nations bring their beavers and other furs. . . . The second is the fertility of the soil. . . . It also has a notable fault which is that it is the most exposed to the blows of . . . the Iroquois and the English, who, not being distant from us, make war upon us . . . .

C

THE MYSTICS: BODY AND SPIRIT

In the following documents, drawn primarily from the writings of Marie de l'Incarnation, the means and ends, material and spiritual, of God's servants in New France are examined.

The description of the Indians by this Ursuline 'Bride of Christ' is of interest not only to the historian but to the anthropologist as well.

The "mores" and "folkways" of the natives are carefully observed. From these letters we learn of the Indians' religious beliefs, and their reactions to the cultural impact of the Europeans.

The material requirements of a religious order in New France, and a tour of the Ursulines' dwelling in Quebec, will be found in Documents 32 and 33. The physical needs of the Church, however, were not an end in themselves: the main concern of the Church of New France, in this period, was the salvation of the natives.

To the mystic, torture and martyrdom were a proof of his choice by God for the fulfilment of the Divine purpose. Suffering and death for the faith were not the end of life, but rather the beginning of eternal happiness in the presence and sight of God. A graphic account of the physical abuse endured by the martyrs is given by Marie de l'Incarnation in a letter to her son. The spiritual sufferings and terrible doubts which afflicted the mystic Chabanel, are recounted in Document 34.

*31. "MARIE DE L'INCARNATION TO MOTHER URSULE . . . SUPERIOR
OF THE URSULINES OF TOURS, QUEBEC, SEPTEMBER 13, 1640"
(Jamet, *Marie de l'Incarnation*, Vol. 3, pp. 201-7).

The demons have conspired, if they can, to destroy the Huron Mission . . . . An old woman . . . of this nation harangued an assembly: "It is the black robes who have caused our deaths. Listen to me and I will prove it. They came to a village where everyone was well; as soon as they were established everyone except three or four died. They moved and the same thing happened. They visited the cabins of other cities and only those into which they did not enter have been exempted from illness or death. Do you not see that when they move their lips, which they call praying, spells come from their mouths . . . . If we do not put them to death promptly they will ruin the whole country . . ." When the woman stopped speaking all concluded that what she said was true and that the evil had to be remedied . . . .

*   *   *

They are sending here Reverend Father Poncet, so that he may recover . . . . We are in sorrow because it has been said that three canoes have been captured by the Iroquois. If this is true, he has been captured, and possibly . . . eaten by now. We will have a . . . martyr in his person which will cause much jealousy amongst others who incessantly look for this great grace.

*32. "MARIE DE L'INCARNATION TO THE SUPERIOR OF THE URSU-
LINES IN FRANCE, QUEBEC, SEPTEMBER 16, 1642"
(Jamet, *Marie de l'Incarnation*, Vol. 3, pp. 270-73).

As you know, Divine Providence has disposed in such a fashion that,
in the last few years, our order has come to the countries of Canada in
order that, within the humble limits of our sex, we might labour for the
Blood of Christ for the souls of those who seemed excluded by barbarism
and ignorance. We know, my Reverend Mother, that the Mothers and
Sisters in France envy, rather than feel compassion for us, in the choice
that God has made of us for so glorious and sublime an enterprise; and
we know also that we were unworthy of this grace . . . .

* * *

But my Reverend Mother, in that which concerns us, . . . we are
compelled to fulfill the functions of our Institute, to provide not only
for the souls but for the bodies as well of those with whom we are entrusted. We must clothe and feed them, which leads me, after having
asked that you succour us by your prayers, to procure a few temporal
commodities. In so doing you will help us cultivate the vine of Our Lord
in these strange lands . . . . If the poor of France move one to tears, I
can assure you that the sight of our poor Indians would make your heart
bleed. . . . In France there are many in need, but at the same time, there
are many to come to their assistance; here all are poor and no one can
help them but us . . . ; but we too are poor and depend on charity for our
necessities.

*33. "MARIE DE L'INCARNATION TO HER SON,
QUEBEC, AUGUST 26, 1644"
(Jamet, *Marie de l'Incarnation*, Vol. 3, pp. 366-85).

. . . The reverend fathers Quentin and Jogues . . . , by a particular
providence of God, were released by the Dutch who inhabit the area near
the Iroquois . . . and were sent to France at the express command of the
Queen. Thus God has rendered to us a veritable martyr, . . . bearing upon
his body the marks of Christ. . . . Imagine the most ignominious things
one can suffer if one is chaste; he suffered them. I do not know if the
relations had, or will, mention them. I will tell you the circumstances
of his travails.

After a frightful bastonade which made him look like a dead beast,
after having cut off two of his fingers and burnt or bitten the rest, they
paraded him naked from village to village . . . before a large assembly
they hung him in the air by the fleshy part of the arms. . . . A barbarian
. . . not able to endure the sight, and with a natural compassion, untied

him when he was nearly dead. After all these torments . . . the Iroquois gave him to a family who took care of him, and held him in affection (meaning that they did him no harm and permitted him to pray to God . . .) ; . . . these people led the Father everywhere they went, and by this means he baptized many sick children and some adults as well. Thus he led many souls to heaven . . . .

In answer to what you want to know of the country, I would inform you, my dear son, that there are stone, wooden, and bark-covered houses. Ours is made all of stone; it is ninety-two feet long and twenty-eight in width; it is the nicest and largest that exists in Canada. . . . Within is the church which is as long as the width of the house and seventeen feet wide. You may think this small but the great frigidity does not permit large buildings. There are times when the priests are in danger of freezing their hands and ears. . . . To maintain an employee costs thirty sols a day and food . . . . We recruit our workers in France on a three-year, or more, contract. We have ten who do all our work. . . . Our house has three stories. We have our cells in the middle story and they are similar to those of France. . . . In winter we cannot long remain in our cells without heat. It would be excessive to remain one hour, and even then we have to keep our hands enfolded or well covered. . . . Our beds are made of wood, and they close as does a cupboard; though we double the blankets . . . we can barely keep warm . . . .

Is our community large? Large enough for the moment. We are eight sisters . . . and a religious domestic. There are four from our Congregation in Tours and four from the Congregation of Paris. The domestic is from Dieppe . . . .

Are our Indians as perfect as I have said? In manners they do not have French forms: by this I mean the ways of paying a compliment or behaving as do the French. We have not spent any time studying these matters, rather we have concentrated on instructing them well in the commandments of God and the Church, all aspects of our faith, all prayers, and the minute examination of all religious matters. An Indian confesses as well as a cleric . . . naïve to extremes, making much of little matters and, if they have erred grievously, they make a public penance with great humility. . . . This year a few got drunk. The elders of the mission, and the Fathers, condemned them to pay a fine of a certain number of beaver skins to be used for the purchase of decorations for the chapel, and they were forbidden to enter the church for three days, besides which, they had to pray twice a day at the church door. . . .

There are Indians as there are Frenchmen. Some are more devout . . . but generally speaking, they are more devout than the French . . . .

34. "DEATH OF CHABANEL, BRESSANI'S RELATION, 1650"
(Thwaites, *Jesuit Relations*, Vol. 40, pp. 37-39).

*   *   *

. . . Father Noel was of the Province of Toulouse. He died at the age of 36 years, 19 in religion, and 6 of residence in those countries, for which he had a strong vocation,—but not indeed, without struggles. After 4 or 5 years of study of those languages, he could hardly make himself understood, although he was not deficient in either talent or memory,—as he had shown in France, where he had taught Rhetoric with great satisfaction. What mortification to a man who burns with zeal, to see himself powerless to produce effect, for want of language! Secondly, he had naturally a great aversion to the manner of life and the customs of the Barbarians — amid the smoke or amid the snows; to lie down on the ground among dogs, and in the almost continual din of great and small, without being able to retreat to any place which was not public; without other light by night than that of a fire full of smoke,—besides the more than daily perils of falling into the hands of an enemy who has for you nothing but fires and unheard-of cruelties. Thirdly, it appeared that God, in order to make his cross heavier, deprived him of visible graces by abandoning him to disgust and sadness. Is not this a great trial, especially if it lasts five or six whole years? Now such was that of this servant of God,—with whom, however, the demon never gained aught. He suggested to him every day, and many times a day, that by returning to France he would find there the contentment which now failed him, both temporal and spiritual, which he had experienced there in the past; that he would there find occupations adapted to his talents and inclination, wherein he would serve God to perfection and with holiness, like so many others,— who were, perhaps, in many respects inferior to himself . . . .

D

THE CANADIEN BOURGEOISIE

Wealth in New France in this period was derived from the fur trade, retail merchandising, and the acquisition of large land grants. The rise of a secular aristocracy in Canada during the French Régime was due to the encompassment of these vital areas of economic activity by an able, vigorous, and favoured class. Political power was another means of achieving, and perpetuating, this privileged position.

The nature of the fur trade, and lay opposition to Jesuit participation in it, are revealed in Lejeune's Relation of 1636. However, the following document, 36, a letter of reference and introduction, indicates one of the sources of power of the favoured class: clerical support.

Another avenue of power and position for the Canadian colonial bourgeoisie was the grant of lands to them by the Company of New France. Influence, then and now, was an imposing asset. The directors of the Company, lacking the money, means, or interest to fulfil the obligations set forth in Document 20, granted extensive seigniories. In return, the seigniors assumed the obligations of clearing the lands, and of bringing over settlers.

The members of the landowning aristocracy, and those who manipulated the fur trade in Canada, were one and the same. They were the secular aristocracy. It was these individuals who formed the Compagnie des Habitants, a Canadian company controlling the fur trade monopoly. They were also the prime movers, and members, of the Council of New France, the first formal, Canadian-based political and economic institution.

Examples of some of the problems facing the *Canadiens* in this period are illustrated in Documents 39 to 41. The proposed treaty between New France and New England was directed against the Iroquois. The inability of the English and French to agree on what constituted a "good" and a "bad" Indian (that is, favourable to the English or favourable to the French) resulted in the treaty's being a proposal, but never an actuality. The two "Ordonnances" are examples of *Canadien* legislation concerning perennial problems of the fur trade.

35. "LEJEUNE'S RELATIONS, 1636"
    (Thwaites, *Jesuit Relations*, Vol. 9, pp. 173-81).

. . . Peltry is not only the best thing and the easiest to make use of in this country, but it is also the coin of the greatest value. And the best of it is that, after it has been used as a covering, it is found to be ready-made gold and silver. You know in France how much consideration is given to the style of a gown. Here all there is to do is to cut it out of a Beaver skin, and the Savage woman straightway sews it to her little child with a moose tendon, with admirable promptness. Whoever wishes to pay in this coin for the goods he buys here, saves thereby the twenty-five per cent that the market price gives them over in France for the risk they run upon the sea. The day-labourers also would rather receive wages for their work in this money. . . . It is for this reason that the Gentlemen of the Company permit to a reasonable extent this practice to everyone, and do not care whether these skins are used for trade, or for protection from the cold,—provided that, in the end, they come back to their store-house, and do not cross the seas except in their own ships. In consequence of this, if occasionally one of them gets into our hands, we do not scruple to use it in the way of a purchase, any more than we would as a covering for the little Savages . . . —or to make for ourselves shoes from the skins of a Moose. . . . This, in truth, is all the profit we derive here from Peltries and other rare things of the Country. . . . If it is dispassionately believed that there is some kind of traffic, or even if Your Reverence deems it best to drop all this, in order not to offend anyone, we are all ready to give it up entirely. . . . But if, on the contrary, you write us that all this is according to God, without semblance of traffic,—although a few slander-ers, about whom we should not trouble ourselves, may stir up their passions at it, and turn it into poison,—we shall not fail to go on, . . . However carefully we have been able to manage things up to the present time, the last letters from that one of our Fathers who handles our income or our charitable gifts over there, . . . indicate that without a little miracle he experienced lately in the assistance of St. Joseph, he would not have been able to furnish us anything this year . . . .

*36. "MARIE DE L'INCARNATION TO HER SON, QUEBEC, SEPTEMBER 15, 1644" (Jamet, *Marie de l'Incarnation,* Vol. 3, pp. 403-5).

I cannot let any occasion pass to write to you without giving myself the satisfaction of doing it. One now presents itself in the form of a very honest gentleman, a lieutenant of the Governor, and a very good friend to us. He (Pierre Le Gardeur de Repentigny) has promised me to see you as he obliges me in everything possible. You will take him for a courtier but you should know that he is very eloquent and of great virtue. His house, which is close to our own, is as ordered as a religious institution. His two daughters board with us. They are two young women who have suckled virtue with their good mother's milk. She is one of the purest souls I have ever known. I tell you this, my dearly beloved son, so that you may honour this good gentleman and to show you that there are good souls in Canada. He is going to France on affairs of the country . . . .

*37. "JUDGMENT BY WHICH HIS MAJESTY APPROVES THE AGREE-MENT . . . BETWEEN THE COMPANY OF NEW FRANCE AND THE INHABITANTS OF NEW FRANCE, OF MARCH 6, 1645. PARIS, JULY 3, 1651" (*Édits et Ordonnances,* pp. 28-29).

... The Company of New France ... grants ..., subject to His
Majesty's pleasure, to the inhabitants of the country ... all rights to the
fur trade in New France ....
    ... the inhabitants of the colony ... will assume ... the expenses
... for the maintenance of the clergy, governor, ... and generally all
charges hitherto assumed by the Company ....

38. "DECREE FOR THE COUNCIL OF NEW FRANCE, 1647"
(P.A.C. *Report*, 1943, pp. xxv-xxvii).

The king being again informed by the Petition of the Directors of the
General Company of New France, that, out of affection towards the
inhabitants of the sd. country, they renounced in favour of the latter
the profit and advantage of the fur trade, having made it over to them at
their insistent request on the conditions contained in the articles agreed
and settled for that purpose approved and ratified by his Maty. Notwithstanding the sd. inhabitants have not gained therefrom all the advantages
hoped for, and having previously undertaken various expenses for the
Conduct of the said trade whereof they had not then all the necessary
experience, they have incurred a number of debts which they have not
been able to pay, And have even had difficulty in meeting the public
charges needful for the maintenance of the colony, especially since some
years ago the said trade with the Indians was thrown open to all the
inhabitants generally, the more so that the more powerful among them
having drawn all the business to themselves and carrying it on to suit
each other, the less favoured who form the majority have gained nothing
by it, notwithstanding all the care taken by the Sr. de Lauzon, governor
of the sd. country. And the price of goods for trade with the Indians has
fallen so low, that short of restoring the trade to the Public stores, for the
greater part at least it would fail altogether in a few years, whereof the
inhabitants have notified them, even offering to restore the said trade to
the said Company, which transfer the Company has not deemed it proper
to accept, knowing by the Course of affairs in the said country and the
report made to them from year to year, that the inhabitants being from
now on well acquainted with the means necessary for the success of the
said trade the sole cause which now deprives them of the result and
advantage which the Country should draw from is that the Community
no longer deals with the public stores, and that certain individuals draw
the profit to themselves alone, and disturb the price fixed for Trade with
the Indians, whereto should it please His Majesty to grant a suitable
remedy for restoring the public stores there would result a profit sufficient
together with the fourth paid by the inhabitants not only to meet the
ordinary charges, but also to cancel the debts of the said country. His

Majesty, wishing to provide for the said petitions and supplications of the said Company, has ordained and ordains that in future, beginning with the present year, all goods suitable for the fur trade with the Indians sent to the sd. country of New France, shall be placed in the public stores, and consigned by the merchants or their agent to the care of the clerks of the sd. Stores appointed by the Council to be formed for the said trade, as will be hereafter explained, his Maty. most strictly forbidding all merchants, agents and others who shall import the said trade goods, to make any other use of them on pain of confiscation thereof, revoking and annulling for this purpose all passports which they have been issued for sending Trade Goods to the said country this present year, Save on condition that those who wish to make use of them shall undertake to carry out the present rule; without power to claim on this account any expenses, loss and interests.

* * *

2

Immediately on the arrival of the Ships in the sd. Country, . . . the goods intended for the trade shall be taken into the public stores of Quebec, Three Rivers and Montreal . . . His Majesty most strictly inhibiting and forbidding the said inhabitants, merchants, agents, Captains, sailors, passengers and all others to trade in any way whatsoever in wine and brandy with the Indians under penalty of corporal punishment.

* * *

4

The said trade Council shall consist of the governor of the Country, of a Director who shall be appointed for three years by the said Company, and of four councillors, two of whom shall be chosen by the Generality of the inhabitants of Quebec likewise by the Generality of the inhabitants of Three Rivers and of Montreal, . . . which four shall have entry, session and deliberative votes in the said trade Council during two consecutive years . . . .

* * *

6

All matters relating to the said trade, the conditions and results thereof, inducing the use of the moneys derived from the fourth and the profit of the trade done in the stores, both for the payment of the ordinary charges, and the extraordinary expenses, shall be debated and decided . . . by a majority of votes . . . , Save that nevertheless the said Council may neither retrench nor diminish the salaries and charges fixed by previous regulations . . . and should there arise any divisions of opinion between the persons who shall form the said Council, In that case the Governor's opinion shall prevail.

39. "LETTER OF THE COUNCIL OF QUEBEC TO THE COMMISSION-
ERS OF NEW ENGLAND, QUEBEC, JUNE 20, 1651"
(O'Callaghan, *Colonial History of the State of New
York*, Vol. 2, pp. 5-7).

. . . It is now several years since the gentlemen of Boston proposed to
us to establish commerce between New France and New England. The
Council constituted by his Majesty in these countries, united their an-
swers to the letters which our Governor had written to your quarter, the
tenor of which was, that we would willingly desire that commerce, and
at the same time the union of hearts and spirits, between your Colonies
and ours, but that we should wish to enter at the same time into a league
offensive and defensive with you against the Iroquois, our enemies, who
would impede us in that trade, or would at least render it less advantageous for you and for us. The obligation which it seems to us you are under
to check the insolence of those Iroquois Savages, who kill the Sokoquis
and the Abenaquis your allies, and moreover, the facility you can enjoy in
this war by taking us the right way, are two reasons which have induced
us to prosecute this matter with you at your Court of Commissioners.
We have requested our Governor to write effectually to you. This is to
unite our entreaties to his, and to assure you of the disposition of our
hearts and of all those of New France, . . . We cannot doubt but God
will bless both your arms and ours, as they will be employed for the
defense of Christian Indians, as well your allies as ours, against barbarous
Heathens, who have neither God nor faith nor any justice in all their
proceedings, as you will be able to learn more at length from the Gentlemen, our said Deputies, who will assure you of the sincere desire we
entertain that Heaven may always go on blessing your Provinces and
heaping its favours, Gentlemen, on you.

*40. "ORDONNANCE OF LAUZON RE TRADING PERMITS, APRIL 28,
1654" (*R.A.P.Q.*, 1924-25, pp. 383-84).

*   *   *

We have learned that a few persons have the intention of going to
trade with the Hurons and other tribes and, as we should know the number and quality of these said persons . . . we forbid all persons of no
matter what station . . . to go and trade without a permit . . . .

*41. "ORDONNANCE OF . . . LAUZON PROHIBITING THE SALE OF
INTOXICATING LIQUOR TO THE INDIANS . . . QUEBEC,
JUNE 20, 1654" (*R.A.P.Q.*,1923-24, p. 384).

> Great disorders among the Indians have appeared due to the liberty
> that Frenchmen have taken of selling or giving them intoxicating liquor
> . . . .
>   On the advice of the Council . . . we . . . prohibit . . the direct or
> indirect sale . . . of . . . liquor to the Indians . . . subject to a penalty . . .
> of a fine . . . or corporal punishment . . . .

E

THE IROQUOIS WARS

The causes of the Iroquois Wars lie not in the Iroquois innate
ferocity, as has sometimes been stated, but rather in the geographic
position and economic policy of the five tribes. There is some evidence
suggesting that the Huron-Iroquois rivalry pre-dates the coming of the
white man. There is, however, no doubt that the settlements of the
Europeans made the rivalry more acute. The homeland of the Iroquois
—roughly the area between Albany and Buffalo in present-day Upper
New York State—lay between the fur-trapping Indians of the hinterland and the Dutch settlements established in 1624. The Iroquois were
the middlemen of a highly lucrative fur trade. Their proximity to the
Dutch, and the latter's desirable iron-age commodities, were the foundation of their economic prosperity.

The Hurons, commercial rivals of the Iroquois, and allies of the
French, menaced the Iroquois' lines of economic communication. The
command of the trade of the tribes of the Great Lakes region, and dominance of the Ottawa River waterway, were the stakes in these intertribal trade wars which took place in three phases: 1641-45, 1648-53, and
1660-67.

A consequence of some significance of these wars was the flaring of
always latent colonial rivalries. The system of alliances was an early
feature of the History of the Americas. The Dutch-Iroquois and, later,
English-Iroquois pacts were countered by the French-Huron and French-
Algonquin compacts. The alliance system would endure until 1760.

The expulsion of the Hurons recounted in Document 42 also resulted in the destruction of the Jesuit Missions in the hinterland. The

highly romanticized martyrdoms also took place: Jogues in 1646, Daniel in 1648, and, in 1650, Brebeuf and Lalemant. At the same time, the returns of the fur trade were substantially reduced. Another result was to expose the colony to direct assault by the Iroquois. Jesuit supplications, fortunately for New France, coincided with the age of Louis XIV and Colbert.

42. "BRESSANI'S RELATION, 1650"
(Thwaites, *Jesuit Relations*, Vol. 40, pp. 45-61).

The cruelty of the Barbarian conqueror of our Christians in their own country threw such a terror into their hearts that many, voluntary exiles, fled to the farthest depth of the woods; others, upon the barren rocks of the fresh-water sea,—preferring precipices and abysses to the fire of the Hiroquois. Others had recourse to a nation which we called "neutral", since it was then at peace with both sides; others, to the mountains of the Tobacco nation. The few who remained exhorted us to stay with them, without retreating farther,—the infidels promising us all to become Christians, and the Christians to be constant in the faith until death . . . .

*   *   *

. . . It is true that the Hurons, before having the light of the Faith, ate the dead bodies of their enemies; but they always had, no less than the Europeans, a horror of eating one another, among their own people. But on this occasion necessity exceeded all laws; a certain brother ate his dead brother; a mother, her dead sons; and the sons, after death, did not recognize or respect the corpses of their own fathers. It was a quite frequent spectacle to see two little children still sucking the dry breasts of their dead mother, the mothers dying with their children in their laps; or to see them die at the breast, which was offered even to the largest, one after the other, to draw thence blood rather than milk,—but with so great and so Christian resignation that it drew from the eyes tears, no less of compassion than of devotion. We have seen the dying come of their own accord to ask from us Baptism, as a passport to the other life, — blessing us at a time when it seemed that impatience should have drawn every malediction from their lips. Many begged us to bury them while still breathing, for fear of being devoured by their people, or at least left naked, — a thing which they esteem more shameful in death than in life. Instructions, sermons, administrations of the Sacraments, were never more frequent; nor had they received with more devotion not only the feasts, but also the working days; these, with visits to the sick and the burial of the dead, were the daily occupations of our Fathers. To these evils were added the fear of the enemies, which caused us to watch whole nights, in order not to be taken unawares, as in the year before. But they, knowing the fortifications that were made, and the vigilance and order which were observed on the Island, turned their arms elsewhere, as was seen. Many who, aided by our alms, escaped the scourge of hunger, were attacked by a contagious disease, which in a few days made great slaughter, especially among the children. There remained nothing but war to ruin them altogether, and this failed not; and thus they were at the same time smitten with all three scourges . . . .

*   *   *

. . . Our only consolation was to take them with us about 300 persons of a nation formerly most populous, but now almost utterly ruined, at the time when it was most faithful to God, — who had drawn from it his elect, and by depopulating the Land, had peopled Heaven, which is enriched by our losses. These unhappy remnants from the divine scourges, did not, in the loss of their possessions, their native Country, and their kinsmen, lose the Faith, — which in this last year had been bestowed by Holy Baptism upon more than three thousand persons; these now enjoy, as we hope, the fruit of it in Paradise. We departed from the Hurons at the beginning of May; and, after 900 miles of march, — amid various hardships and perils, and frequent shipwrecks, — we all finally arrived in perfect health, on the 28th of July, 1650, at Kebec, — whither, soon afterwards, about 300 others followed us . . . .

43. "RELATION OF 1659-1660"
(Thwaites, *Jesuit Relations*, Vol. 45, pp. 211-15).

*   *   *

. . . And as for cruelty, I would make this paper blush, and my listeners would shudder, if I related the horrible treatment inflicted by the Agnieronnons upon some of their captives. This has indeed been mentioned in other relations; but what we have recently learned is so strange that all that has been said on the subject is nothing. I pass over these matters, not only because my pen has no ink black enough to describe them, but much more from a fear of inspiring horror by recounting certain cruelties never heard of in past ages.

It is only a neat trick with them to make a cut around the thumb of a captive, near the first joint; and then, twisting it, to pull it off by main strength, together with the sinew, which usually breaks towards he elbow or near the shoulder, so great is the violence employed. The thumb, thus removed with its sinew, is hung to the sufferers ear like an earpendant, or attached to his neck in place of a carcanet. Then they will do the same with a second and a third finger, while, to replace the fingers that have been pulled off, they force into the wounds splinters of hard wood, which causes pain quite different from the foregoing, although excessive, and very soon produces a great inflammation and a huge swelling of the entire hand and even of the whole arm. Even if this first game were all, is it not with reason that the French of this country have so long asked the destruction of so cruel an enemy? since, after all, five or six hundred men are unable to withstand a courageous undertaking, if it be executed in such a manner as the glory of God and the compassion due to them demand. The Iroquois have the disposition of women; there are none more courageous when no resistance is offered them, and none more cowardly when they encounter opposition. They deride the French, because they have never seen them wage war in their country; and the French have never done so because they have never made the attempt, hitherto, believing the roads more difficult to pass than they really are. With our present knowledge of these barbarians, — having seen, since we were in their midst, how alarm was everywhere felt when they beheld themselves attacked in their own country, — it must be said with full assurance that, if an army of five hundred Frenchmen should arrive unexpectedly, it could say "Veni, vidi, vici."

F

THE NEW ORDER: LAVAL

The accomplishments of the Jesuit missionaries from 1625 to 1659 were, to say the least, minor. However, the failure of their missions was more than compensated for by their activities as secular colonial agents.

One of their greatest contributions to Canadian society was yet to come: the erection of a Canadian Roman Catholic Church. The choice of their candidate, François de Montmorency-Laval, as head of the Canadian Mission, and, in 1674, as Bishop of Quebec, had far-reaching effects. Laval laid the foundations of the Roman Catholic structure of French Canada.

It would be a dangerous distortion, however, to overestimate Laval's power. He was opposed, as had been the Jesuits, by the secular aristocracy, other religious orders, and by the State. In New France, Church-State conflicts but reflected the Gallican-Ultramontane controversies of Old France. In Canada this was manifested in lay resistance, and open quarrels between the representatives of the King and the Church.

44. "LALLEMANT TO RENAULT, QUEBEC, SEPTEMBER 12, 1659"
(Thwaites, *Jesuit Relations*, Vol. 45, p. 35).

* * *

... However, although all these things augur nothing but disasters for
us, we cannot doubt that God has high purposes with respect to these
lands, in order to derive glory from them. For he has revived our hopes
by the gift which he had made us of a Prelate for whom this incipient
Church has been sighing so long, — that is, Monseigneur the Bishop of
Petraea, who happily arrived here on the 16th day of June, 1659 . . . .

45. "JOURNAL OF THE JESUIT FATHERS IN THE YEARS 1659, 1660
AND 1661" (Thwaites, *Jesuit Relations*, Vols. 45-46,
pp. 81, 161-63, 165).

APRIL 1659

9) The habitans of beaupré presented a petition to Monseigneur
the governor to have an inquiry made respecting the life and morals of
Monsieur Vaillant, a priest of the said côte. The petition was referred to
the officiality.

10) A petition was presented to Monsieur the Governor by Monsieur
Vaillant, requesting that inquiry be made against the said habitants as
calumniators. The petition was granted, and Monsieur Chartier with his
Clerk was sent in the capacity of commissioner, by Monsieur the Governor, to the Côte de Beaupré to hold an Inquiry. He examined 83 wit-
nesses.

Monsieur the governor, after examining the Evidence given at the
Inquiry, referred the matter to the official, and condemned the said Sieur
Vaillant to pay the costs.

NOVEMBER 1660

On the 5th sailed the last ship — that of Pointel, on board of which
were Monsieur Charon, Villeré, and others.

On the 7th, a huron arrived who had escaped from Agniée; he con-
firmed the news of an army.

On the 28th, Monseigneur the Bishop held a meeting of the churchwardens, and stated that Monsieur the Governor was no longer an hon-
ourary Churchwarden; and this without having told him of it. On the
30th following, Monsieur the Governor was present at the meeting of
the churchwardens, with his usual suite; and there he asserted his right
to maintain himself in his office, declaring to Monseigneur the Bishop
that he had not the power to remove him. Several words were said that
were not very respectful to the position of Monseigneur the Bishop,
which gave rise to dissatisfaction on both sides.

FEBRUARY 1661

. . . Monsieur the Governor and Monseigneur the Bishop were present, and, as Monsieur the Governor had stated that he would not attend
if Monseigneur the Bishop were saluted before him, we induced him to
agree that the children's hands should be kept occupied, so that neither
one nor the other would be saluted, both at the Prologue and at the
Epilogue. The Children were notified and commanded to do this; but the
children, who were Charles Couillard and Ignace de repentigny, insti-
gated and persuaded by their parents, did just the contrary, and saluted
Monsieur the Governor first. This greatly offended Monseigneur the
Bishop. We tried to appease him; and the two children were whipped,
on the following morning, for having disobeyed.

At the same time, the churchwardens were deprived of their place in
the procession, and the gentlemen — or self-styled thus — were put in
front of them, after Monsieur the Governor. This gave rise to trouble,
which resulted in the Interdiction of the processions.

G

THE NEW ORDER: THE KING

The development of New France to date has been characterized by a
semi-involvement of the French State in the affairs of the colony. In
1663, the fledgling is taken under the Royal wing there to remain, for
better or worse, until 1760.

The "Instructions to Gaudais", a sort of Royal Commission on
Colonial Affairs, indicates future trends: first, an assessment; then
recommendations; and finally, in the period to follow, the implementation of the New Order.

*46. "RENUNCIATION OF THE COMPANY OF NEW FRANCE, PARIS,
MARCH 1663" (*Édits et Ordonnances*, pp. 31-32).

Since it has pleased God to bring peace to our Kingdom our main
interest has been the re-establishment of commerce, this being the principal means of abundance . . . and as the greater part of this abundance

arises from our colonial establishments we have . . . turned our eyes to
New France . . . where, to our regret, we see few inhabitants established
. . . and these are in daily danger . . . from the Iroquois . . . as the remnants of the One Hundred Associates . . . are not in a position to furnish
the necessary colonists . . . nor to defend them, we have resolved . . . to
accept the renunciation of their charter . . . .

LOUIS . . .

*47. "INSTRUCTIONS TO GAUDAIS, PARIS, MAY 7, 1663"
(*Ordonnances et Jugements,* Vol. 3, pp. 23-27).

The first matter which the Sieur Gaudais must remember . . . is the
continuous and particular . . . application necessary for the fulfilment of
the matters contained in these instructions.

First he must obtain accurate information on the country: how many
degrees it is from the pole? The length of the days and nights; the good
or bad qualities of the air. The regularity or irregularity of the seasons
and the general lay of the land. After these first considerations, he
should carefully inform himself of the fertility of the land . . . .

. . . it would be well to describe the three habitations of Quebec,
Montreal, and Three Rivers; the number of families in the habitations;
the number of souls of both sexes; to what, in particular, the inhabitants
apply themselves? In what consists their commerce and the means of
sustenance available? And how they bring up their children?

And as it is obvious . . . that the prosperity and development of the
country is impossible withot concentrating the areas of settlement . . .
he will try and convince . . . the Bishop, Governor, and principal inhabitants of the country . . . of the necessity of gathering the inhabitants
into areas of close settlement . . . .

The . . . Sieur Gaudais will note if the country lacks women or girls
so that provisions may be made for sending some in the coming years . . . .

The principal menace to the inhabitants of the country being the
Iroquois, who at all moments attack the French . . . and massacre them
cruelly, . . . the King has resolved, if it is necessary, to send next year
some regular troops to the country . . . The Sieur Gaudais will examine
with great care the number of men required, munitions and food needed,
and the supplies and help that may be expected from within the country
itself . . . .

And as the main source of revenue consisted of the fur trade . . .
which has been found to be damaging to the interests of the country, as
the inhabitants apply themselves to the trade rather than, as in the past,
to the development of agriculture, the King wishes the Sieur Gaudais to
inform himself by what means His Majesty may derive the profit from the

said trade and to inform the inhabitants that it is their welfare he wishes
. . . and that he would contribute substantial sums every year to their
maintenance . . . .

The Sieur Gaudais will inform himself if, in the country, there are
iron deposits; what they would produce should they be developed by the
King or by some individuals to whom a concession might be granted. . . .
What must be even more clearly verified is if there are prodigious quantities of trees of great height of which masts could be made . . . .

LOUIS
DE LIONNE

PART III

1663-1713

In Parts I and II, the activities of the men and women in the nascent Canadian society have been rather arbitrarily classified as A, B, and C: man as a political animal, man as an economic animal, and man as a religious animal. In fact, man, in the complexity of his being, is political, material, and religious all at the same time. It must be remembered that the neat little categories erected by the historian are a tool of comprehension and not a reality in themselves.

A further threat to accurate comprehension manifests itself in the period 1663 to 1713: that of presenting and interpreting documents from the pens of the *great men*, the heroes of the French Régime, such as Louis XIV, Talon, and Frontenac. Descriptions of the era of Louis XIV as one of a benevolent despotism; of Talon as ambitious and industrious, or of Frontenac as haughty and brave, obscure a significant, and sometimes overlooked, feature of the period. These men were the ruler, intendant, and governor of New France, but also *in* New France. It is a truism that these men deeply influenced Canadian society. It should be another truism that the needs and structures of the society influenced them.

Royal government in New France was something old and something new, old in that prior structures were the foundations for France built on the work of Champlain, the Jesuits, and the secular aristocracy. It modified, but did not create anew, the economic and political institutions. The novelty of Crown government lay in the integration of the colony into the French imperial scheme, and the capital resources of the metropolis now at the disposal of New France.

The reorganization of the colony encompassed civil, economic, demographic, religious, and military affairs. All these are considered in general, as well as in a particular manner in the first theme. The powers, scope, actions, and reactions of the Sovereign Council, intendant, and governor, it will be evident, defy simple classification. Because of its complexity the first theme, unlike those which follow, embraces the whole of Canadian society rather than a part.

A

ROYAL GOVERNMENT: POLITICAL,

MATERIAL, MILITARY, AND SOCIAL

ORGANIZATION

1. THE INTENDANT:

Talon, the first intendant to come to New France, was a French civil servant. As such, he served in Canada from 1665 to 1668 and from 1670 to 1672.

The theoretical line of demarcation between the powers of the intendant and those of the governor was that civil matters were the concern of the former, and military affairs the concern of the latter. Talon's commission should, however, be compared to that of the governor. A conflict of powers was a decided possibility.

The extensive powers granted to French government officials in the colony tended to be mitigated by two factors. One was the Sovereign or Superior Council (both designations are used in Document 48), the majority of whose members were Canadians, and chosen from the secular aristocracy. The second factor was that if the transient Crown official hoped to implement his plans he had to have the support and co-operation of the Canadians.

The interaction between colonial needs, the ability of one man, and a far-seeing metropolitan government are illustrated in Documents 50 to 53. Colbert, the French Minister of Marine, and the intendant's superior, indicates an awareness and concern for the colony's problems in his instructions to Talon. The means of solving these are the substance of Talon's reports.

*48. "EDICT CREATING THE SUPERIOR COUNCIL OF QUEBEC, PARIS, APRIL 1663" (*Édits, Ordonnances Royaux,* Vol. 1, pp. 37-39).

. . . we have resolved . . . that the prosperity of the country . . . and the well-being . . . of our subjects . . . depends on the establishment of laws, this being the principal means, and a necessary prelude . . . in the administration of government . . ., and aware that the great distance of the country from our Kingdom . . . precludes a prompt settlement of pressing problems . . . , [We] believe that no better means may be found than to establish laws and a Sovereign Council . . . the said council to be composed of . . . de Mézy, governor and representative of our person, De Laval, Bishop of Petraea, or the senior cleric . . . , and five others whom they will choose jointly; . . . and an Attorney-General. . . . The five persons chosen will be appointed on a yearly basis, . . . To the council . . . we grant to the power . . . to hear all civil and criminal cases . . . in conformity to the laws of our Kingdom . . . reserving to ourselves, however, . . . the right to amend and reform the . . . laws. . . . The said council will regulate the dispersement of all public moneys, the fur trade . . . and any other commerce involving the inhabitants of the country and the merchants of our Kingdom, . . . In addition . . . the council may establish at Quebec, Montreal, and Three Rivers, lower courts . . . .

And . . . for the preservation of the debates, edicts, and judgments, . . . the council . . . will make provisions for a recording clerk . . . .

LOUIS

*49. "COMMISSION OF INTENDANT OF JUSTICE, POLICE AND FINANCE IN CANADA, ACADIA, NEWFOUNDLAND AND OTHER LANDS OF FRANCE IN THE NORTH FOR M. TALON, PARIS, MARCH 23, 1665" (*Ordonnances et Jugements,* Vol. 3, pp. 33-35).

*   *   *

In that, for the well-being of our people and the establishment of justice, police, and finance in our lands of Canada, it is necessary to establish in the office of intendant . . . a person capable of serving us with dignity, we have, to this end, chosen you because of the particular trust we have in your experience, good conduct, and integrity, which are

qualities that you have proved on all occasions when they were required
. . . .

For these reasons, and others . . . we appoint you . . . by these present
signed by our hand, intendant of justice, police, and finance . . . and in
that function [you] will assist at the Councils of War to be held by our
Governor-General in America, and by the Governor in Canada. You will
hear . . . all complaints made to you by our peoples in the said countries
. . . of excesses, injuries, and violences, and render them proper and
expeditious justice. You will also inform yourself of any and all practices
and enterprises . . . against our service. Take action against the guilty of
any crime whatsoever no matter what their standing; initiate and complete proceedings until a definitive judgment has been rendered and
executed. . . . In the absence of our Governor-General . . . and the Governor . . . you will preside over the Sovereign Council. . . . In civil matters
you will be the sovereign judge and in such matters may issue ordonnances as you see fit which we, as of now, validate, as well as for the
future . . . .

It is also our wish that you supervise the expenditures . . . and distribution of the funds destined . . . for the maintenance of men of war, as
well as the munitions, reparations, fortifications, . . . loans, and contributions . . . made for our service . . . .

                                                                LOUIS

Read and published by the Sovereign Council . . . at Quebec, September 23, 1665 . . . and registered . . . .

                                                            PEUVRET

*50. "MEMOIR OF THE KING TO SERVE AS INSTRUCTIONS TO TALON,
PARIS, MARCH 27, 1665" (*R.A.P.Q.*, 1930-31, pp. 11-20).

●   ●   ●

. . . Talon should know that those who have written the most accurate
and disinterested reports on the said country have always said that the
Jesuits, whose piety and zeal have greatly contributed to attracting the
people presently established, have assumed an authority which surpasses
that necessary to the fulfilment of their veritable profession. . . . To
maintain themselves . . . they have named the Bishop of Petraea, who is
dependent upon them, to fulfil the episcopal functions. And, to date.
when they have named the King's Governor, . . . they have used every
means to revoke those named for this task without their participation,
so that, as it is absolutely necessary to maintain a just balance between
the temporal authority which belongs to the person of the King, and the
spiritual, which belongs to the person of the said Bishop and the Jesuits,
in a manner, however, that the latter be inferior to the former, the said
Talon . . . will observe, and acquire a knowledge of, the present con-

ditions of the two authorities in the country . . . without . . . , however, disclosing his motives.

* * *

Since the year 1662 [sic] His Majesty has joined the said country to the concession made to the Company of the West Indies. It is necessary that the said . . . Talon examine the titles of concession by which the Company has the right to name the Governor and other officials; and as the Company knows well enough that it is incapable of finding persons of sufficient merit and authority to occupy these posts . . . it has accepted that the King make these appointments . . . .

* * *

As the colony may derive a considerable advantage from the establishment of beneficial regulations . . . concerning the administration of public funds, agriculture, as well as the industries we may establish . . . , Talon, in concert with the officials of the . . . Council, and the principal inhabitants of the country, will take means to establish fixed regulations on this subject, and see that they are observed, and founding them, if possible, on those established . . . in the cities of the Kingdom. . . . A statement of the revenues of the country has been given him as well as the uses to which they have been put to date, and the debts which have been contracted together with the annual interest due. . . . It is the intention of the King . . . that he acquire a precise knowledge of the matters . . . .

* * *

He will observe that one of the greatest needs of Canada is the establishment of industries and the attraction of artisans capable of producing the necessities of life, for, to date, it has been necessary to import cloth to clothe the inhabitants, and even shoes for their use either because they were obliged to cultivate the soil as their sole and most important occupation, or because of the lack of zeal and industry of those who have governed to date. It is for these reasons that he will examine all possible means for the introduction of so useful a thing in the said country to which His Majesty will contribute by opening his coffers, being persuaded that a large sum of money could not be better employed.

* * *

Once the expedition against the Iroquois is terminated, the King wishes the said . . . Talon to invite the soldiers . . . of the Carignan Regiment, as well as the four infantry companies . . . to remain in the country, and to grant to each of them a small gratuity in His Majesty's name in order that they may have the means of establishing themselves . . . .

LOUIS

*51. "TALON TO COLBERT, QUEBEC, NOVEMBER 13, 1666"
(*R.A.P.Q.*, 1930-31, pp. 54-62).

I will no longer write to you of the great establishments that I believe
possible in Canada for the glory and utility of the King and state, as you
believe that there are not in France enough surpluses and useful subjects
to populate New France. . . . I will give my care, and all my application,
to that which you have ordered me until such time as the matter appears
to you worthy of greater support than accorded this year . . . .

* * *

I am working as hard as I can to reunite and consolidate the distant
habitations, and I oppose future settlement in any form other than a
community, hamlet, village, or borough. To show that it is feasible I
have undertaken to form three villages in the vicinity of Quebec which
are already well advanced. I am reserving two for the families you plan
on sending this year, for according to the instructions I have received,
I must prepare forty dwellings. The third consists of 18 of the most
worthy of consideration of the troops: . . . le Chevalier de Chaumont, the
general agent of the company; 6 captains of the Carignan-Salières regiment and 10 subalterns, as well as . . . de Tracy's secretary, have undertaken to each establish a dwelling and this will stimulate others. As I
borrowed from the Jesuit Fathers, and a few individuals, the land I have
occupied, one can leave them the seigniorial possession and the rights
due, unless His Majesty would rather establish here a king's domain and
thus assure to himself the benefits of the new settlers in the manner I
suggested in a project which I forwarded to my brother. . . . By this I
would find the means to garrison the Fort of St. Louis, or by establishing
a king's domain, eventually render the country self-supporting.
. . . hemp grows well in this country. I have had it sown and reaped
at different locations. . . . I am sending some to . . . de Terron as a
sample, and to my brother to show you, if you so desire. I have no doubts
that some day much will be produced here and more than in Lower
Brittany.
The newly cleared lands have appeared better to me because of the
care that was taken. When I distributed the seeds I had brought last
year, I insisted that a like amount be returned to me at the present harvest and this has been done, so that I give what is returned to those in
need, and on the same conditions. . . . One could well send over seed
from France, but by the time it reaches here it is old and does not produce at all. I have found that to encourage the inhabitants to grow a
great deal of hemp it was necessary to reduce them to want thread. To
this end I seized all that I could find here and I will only distribute it to
those who agree to return a stated quantity of hemp . . . .

* * *

To encourage the inhabitants to undertake the construction of a couple of vessels . . . I have had one begun this winter. . . . To finance the work I have used the . . . two thousand écus which I received from the sale of the supplies I had bought . . . that the King had the goodness to let me bring over without paying any shipping charges . . . .

I have had cod fishing begun in the River and I know that it will be abundant and profitable. I even hope that sedentary establishments may be made, for it would be of double benefit for, in winter, the crews could hunt for moose.

One of the great advantages that I see in this country is that it may some day, if it is well populated, furnish a large number of sailors as the inhabitants have a great and close disposition to navigation.

* * *

If the King accommodated Holland by stipulating, to England, the necessity of restoring New Holland to the former, and prior to this found the means of negotiating with the Gentlemen of the Estates, I believe an agreement could be reached on reasonable terms. . . . This would be of benefit to the King, giving him two entries into Canada and also . . . all the peltries of the North from which the English now derive profit . . . by the relations they have with the Iroquois. . . . It would also place these barbarian nations under the discretion of His Majesty and, besides which, New Sweden could also be obtained . . . and this would keep New England contained within its limits . . . .

TALON

*52. "MEMOIR OF TALON ON THE PRESENT STATE OF CANADA, 1667" (*R.A.P.Q.*, 1930-31, pp. 63-66).

Canada is a vast country of different elevations capable, in its . . . climates, and exposures to the sun, of producing all that does Old France. Like her, there is heat in the South, cold in the North, and temperateness in the middle of the extremes. There are many natural prairies which produce an abundance of grass, and of such good quality that all sorts of livestock might be well fattened.

It is fertile in Frenchmen . . . women bear almost every year as do animals native to the country. The same does not apply to the Indians whose women are somewhat sterile either because of the onerous work they must do which restricts bearing, or because they nourish too long their children with their milk, but this obstacle to the rapid growth of the Colony may be overcome by a few regulations easy to introduce and implement . . . .

The colony of Canada may aid by her productions the subsistence of the Antilles and become an assured source of assistance should that of

France fail. This help may be in flour, vegetables, fish, wood, oil, and other things not yet discovered.

*53. "TALON TO COLBERT, QUEBEC, OCTOBER 10, 1665"
(*R.A.P.Q.*, 1930-31, p. 40).

P.S.: If I use a borrowed hand to write . . . it is because my hand-writing is not as polished as this one. In this . . . I mean no mark of disrespect. I humbly request, once and for all, that you approve that I may continue so in the future.

2. TALON AND DEMOGRAPHIC COLONIZATION

It would be an exaggeration to attribute to Talon the sole credit for the rapid increase of the population of New France in this period. There were other factors at work. One of these, and an important one, was the French Minister of Marine, Jean-Baptiste Colbert. This able and industrious councillor of Louis XIV rationalized the colonial administration of France and provided Talon with the metropolitan support essential to a successful colonial endeavour. In this case it was men, and women, rather than merely money.

The paucity of human resources, native and French, was a constantly heard complaint in Canada. France, by its restrictive laws, discouraged non-Catholic immigration. However, it should be noted that New France itself had little to attract settlers. Suitable immigrants from France were loath to leave their prosperous and civilized homeland for the wilds of the North American continent.

A limited sponsored immigration to New France took place during Talon's régime. Other means used by the State to increase the population were the payment, to young men and women, of a King's dowry, a tax on bachelors and a progressive baby-bonus scheme as a reward for fertility. Population growth, however, was slow throughout the French Régime, and even this growth was the result of the efforts of the Canadians rather than of the French State.

The summary of the census of 1666 and the professions of Canadians in Document 58 illustrate another aspect of the reorganization of New France. The census was a means of determining not only the number of citizens, but their occupations, progress in industry and agriculture, number of domestic animals, seigniories, government buildings, churches and so on. These statistical records indicate numerically the development of Canadian society.

*54. "COLBERT TO TALON, VERSAILLES, JANUARY 5, 1666"
   (R.A.P.Q., 1930-31, pp. 41-46).

*   *   *

His Majesty cannot concur in all the reasons you put forward for
the formation of Canada into a great and powerful state finding that
there are divers obstacles that could only be surmounted by the passage
of many years. Even granting that there were no other concerns and
that the resources of the Kingdom . . . could be applied to Canada, it
would not be prudent to depopulate his Kingdom . . . to populate
Canada.

                                                        COLBERT

*55. "ABRIDGED CENSUS OF THE . . . FAMILIES IN NEW FRANCE,
   1666" *(R.A.P.Q.*, 1935-36, pp. 153-54).

Quebec	555
Beaupré	678
Beauport	172
Ile d'Orléans	471
St. Jean, St. François, and	
St. Michel	156
Sillery	217
Nôtre Dame des Anges and the	
St. Charles River	118
Côte de Lauzon	6
Montreal	584
Three Rivers	461
Total	3,418

Number of men capable of bearing arms between the ages of 16 and
   50 . . . : 1,344.
There are, without doubt, some omissions . . . which will be corrected
   in the winter of 1666.

                                                        TALON

*56. "DECREE OF THE KING'S COUNCIL FOR THE ENCOURAGEMENT
   OF MARRIAGES . . . IN CANADA, APRIL 1, 1670"
   (Édits, Ordonnances Royaux, Vol. 1, pp. 67-68).

. . . it is ordered . . . that in the future all inhabitants of the . . .

country who have up to ten legitimate children living who are neither priests nor belong to any religious order . . . will be paid . . . a yearly gratuity of three hundred livres, and those who have twelve, four hundred livres; . . . In addition . . . it is the King's will . . . that all males who marry before the age of twenty, and females before the age of sixteen, will receive on their wedding day twenty livres to be known as the King's gift . . . .

COLBERT

*57. "COLBERT TO TALON, FEBRUARY 11, 1671" (*R.A.P.Q.*, 1930-31, pp. 143-48).

*   *   *

The King has heard with pleasure . . . that of the 165 women who came last year there remained but 15 to be married . . . and that the soldiers, having worked on the habitations, are capable of marrying. To this effect His Majesty has taken the measures necessary to send 150 women this year. I am sure that as soon as they arrive you will see that they are established and married to . . . soldiers and other inhabitants. . . . You did well to order that volunteers would be deprived of the right to engage in the fur trade and hunt unless they married within 15 days of the arrival of the vessels bringing the women.

With regard to those who will make the trip this year I have given the necessary orders so that those chosen will be healthy and strong . . . .

58. "PROFESSIONS IN CANADA, 1681" (*Census of Canada*, Vol. 4, p. 13).

Archers	1	Armourers	2
Land Surveyors	2	Gunsmiths	11
Butchers	8	Bakers	7
Hotel Keepers	1	Calkers	1
Artillerymen	1	Carders	1
Braziers	3	Hatters	6
Wheelwrights	14	Carpenters	56
Ships Carpenters	4	Surgeons	13
Shoemakers	26	Rope Makers	4
Cutler	1	Roofer	5
Blacksmiths	4	Cook	2
Masons	30	Bailiffs	3
Farrier	2	Merchants	7
Joiners	24	Sailors	8

Notaries	24	Millers	2
Fitters	1	Confectioners	2
Wooden Shoemaker	8	Powder Makers	1
Saddler	1	Locksmiths	6
Tailors	34	Edge Tool Maker	17
Carpet Weavers	1	Tanners	5
Weavers	4	Riband Weaver	1
Turners	4	Coopers	9
		Vinegar Makers	1

3. MARTIAL ORGANIZATION

We have seen that just prior to the establishment of Royal Government, New France was faced with a serious military threat. By destroying the Hurons, the Iroquois had removed a threat to their flank. They made bold incursions into the very heart of the colony. Montreal was perpetually in a state of siege and even the area about Quebec City felt the blows of the Iroquois warriors. The perpetual crisis retarded agriculture, severely restricted the returns of the fur trade, and endangered the very survival of the colony.

In addition to the threat of the Iroquois, the period is noteworthy for the introduction of a new constant in the history of the French Régime: in 1664 the English were ceded New Amsterdam by the Dutch. It is to this event that Talon refers in Document 51. The English colony was named New York. The new neighbours of the Iroquois replaced the Dutch as the purveyors of European goods. In return the English became the recipients of the benefits of the Iroquois commercial system. The European-Indian alliances which would characterize the balance of the French Régime in Canada were established.

Documents 59 and 60 are concerned with the termination of the First Iroquois Wars. The readings which follow indicate the means used by the French government to organize the inhabitants of New France for purposes of defence. The metropolis supplied some regular troops, but the colony was expected to contribute as well. Compulsory military service was the solution and service in the militia for the defence of New France was an accepted obligation.

Although no document is included in this section on the Indian warriors serving with the French regulars and the Canadian militia, their contributions to the defence of Canada should be noted. On the whole the French had better relations with the indigenous peoples than did the English. One reason for this was the work of the missionaries. However, the requirements of the fur trade and New France's small

population were also factors. In few words, the French needed the allies
far more than did the English.

> 59. "OF THE WAR AND THE TREATIES OF PEACE OF THE FRENCH
> WITH THE IROQUOIS, 1666" (O'Callaghan, *Documentary
> History of the State of New York*, Vol. 1, pp. 46-49).

The great varieties of Nations which are in this country, the change-
able and perfidious dispositions of the Iroquois and the barbarism of all
these tribes not permitting us to hope for any stable peace with them
except inasmuch as it can be maintained by the terror of the King's
arms, it is not to be wondered at that peace succeeds war so easily, and
that wars terminate so quickly in peace.

*   *   *

However as no advantage can be expected from these nations except
in so far as we appear able to injure them, preparations were made for
a military expedition against those with whom no peace could be concluded. Monsieur de Courcelle, who commanded, used every possible
diligence so that he was ready to start on the 9th of January of the year
1666 accompanied by M. du Gas, whom he took for his Lieutenant;
by Monsieur de Salamper, Gentlemen Volunteer; by Father Pierre Raf-
feix, Jesuit; by 300 men of the Regiment of Carignan Salières, and 200
Volunteers, habitans of the French Colonies . . . .

A more difficult or longer march than that of this little army, can
scarcely be met with in any history, and it required a French courage and
the perseverance of M. de Courcelle, to undertake it. In addition to the
embarrassment caused by the snow shoes, which is a species of great
inconvenience and that of the burthen which each one was obliged to
carry, it was necessary to walk three hundred leagues on the snow; cross
lakes and rivers continually on the ice in danger of making as many falls
as steps; sleep only on the snow in the midst of the forest and endure a
cold surpassing by many degrees in severity that of the most rigorous
European winters.

*   *   *

The effects of the terror produced by his Majesty's arms on the hearts
of these savages were apparent at Quebec in the month of May following, by the arrival of ambassadors from the Senecas, who demanded the
King's protection . . . .

These treaties had not, however, all the success which was expected
from them, and M. de Tracy, concluded that, to ensure their success,
it was necessary to render the Mohawks by force of arms more tractable.

*   *   *

60. "TALON TO COLBERT, NOVEMBER 13, 1666"
(O'Callaghan, *Documentary History of the State of New York*, Vol. 1, p. 54).

Monsieur de Tracy and Monsieur de Courcelle are returned from their expedition, the Iroquois having concluded to retreat and abandon their settlements. The said M. de Tracy could do nothing else than burn their forts and lay waste everything. These two gentlemen will inform you of whatever occurred throughout their march which occupied fifty-three days. What I learn from public opinion is that in what has been performed nothing has been left undone, and that the King's orders had been executed and his expectations entirely realized had those savages stood their ground. It would, in truth, have been desirable that a part had been defeated and some others taken prisoners.

The advanced age of M. de Tracy must greatly enhance the merit of the service he has rendered the King, by assuming in a broken-down frame such as his, a fatigue of which no correct idea can be formed. I am assured that throughout the whole march of three hundred leagues, including the return, he would suffer himself to be carried only during two days, and then he was forced to do so by the gout. M. de Courcelle, though stronger than he, could not help being carried in a like manner, having been attacked by a contraction of the nerves. Both in truth have endured all the fatigue that human nature is capable of.

*61. "THE KING TO M. DE COURCELLE ON THE DIVISION OF THE INHABITANTS OF CANADA INTO MILITIA COMPAGNIES, PARIS, APRIL 3, 1669" (P.A.C. *Report*, 1940-41, p. 8).

. . . you will note my intention to favour marriages, and reward my subjects who have ten to twelve children . . . by the decree of my council which will be presented by my Attorney-General to the Sovereign Council of New France. As the prosperity and maintenance of the country requires more than a rational demographic policy . . . I write you these lines to state that it is our will that you divide . . . the male subjects of the country into companies . . . and that after having so divided them that you appoint Captains, Lieutenants and ensigns to comand them, . . .

I will leave to your prudence whether it would be advisable for the well-being of our state, and the aggrandizement of the colony, to assemble every two or three years 1,200 well-armed soldiers and to lead them into the lands of the Iroquois and other Indian nations so that they may be

impressed by the strength of our arms and to maintain them in the
obedience and duties which they owe us.

LOUIS

COLBERT

*62. "ORDONNANCE ON THE WITHHOLDING, BY AN OFFICER, OF A
SOLDIER'S PAY, 1686-1687(?)" (*Mandements des Évêques*,
Vol. 1, pp. 189-90).

With reference to the case proposed: how should a confessor conduct
himself towards officers who withhold the pay of their soldiers, we are
convinced of the following:
   . . . they have no right by law to withhold the pay of their soldiers
albeit they do have the right to confine them to their quarters. . . . From
this it follows that the soldiers must make a free gift of it, which would
protect the officer. If then the soldier, to gain the consent of their captains to work off the limits of their quarters so that they will have the
means of earning more than their pay, freely concede their pay, the said
officers, in good conscience, may accept it.
   However, if they use threats, constraints, . . . and other menaces . . .
to force the soldiers to give up their pay . . . it is an injustice . . . .
   And as it is difficult to control in practice, for most soldiers freely
offer to lose their pay, one must, as much as possible, make these gentlemen promise not to withhold the pay in the future.

JEAN . . . [ST.-VALLIER]

*   *   *

4. FRONTENAC

The best-known governor of Canada during the French Régime is
without a doubt Frontenac. He was governor from 1672 to 1682 and
from 1689 until his death in 1698. "The Fighting Governor", as he has
been called, deserved the appellation: he fought with the intendant,
the Governor of Montreal, whom he jailed at one point, the Bishop,
the Jesuits, the members of the Sovereign Council, and occasionally,
during his second term, with the Iroquois. However, to be critical of
some of the interpretations of Frontenac is not to deny his influence
on the society he was called upon to govern.
   From 1672 to 1675 his authority in the colony was unchecked. Talon
had returned to France, Laval was also in France, and the governor was
many miles from the restraining influence of Colbert and the King.

For three years he was the supreme military and civil administrator of the colony. The effects of his policies had economic, political, religious, social, and military repercussions.

The new governor arrived at an auspicious time. Great strides had been made in industry and commerce during Talon's terms of office. Peace had been established as a result of the campaigns of Tracy and de Courcelle. The basic structures of the society were erected and functioning. His commission, Document 63, granted him extensive powers to maintain these favourable conditions. At the same time, he was advised that he should not rely too much on help from France. The policy of the metropolis at this point was to insist on a slow, orderly development of the colony.

Frontenac, however, initiated a policy of rapid expansion. Documents 65 to 67 indicate his motives and the means he used to implement his policies. The construction of Fort Frontenac on the shores of Lake Ontario had effects that reverberated throughout French Canada. As a military establishment the post protected the allies of the French and threatened the warriors of the Iroquois, but also their trade lines. The location of the fort, and the fur-trading right granted to its seignior, LaSalle, menaced the commerce of the traders of Montreal. It was rumoured that the seignior of the fort and Frontenac were partners. Fénelon's sermon, Document 68, illustrates the resentment of the Montrealers at this foul blow to their commerce. Louis XIV's and Colbert's opinions are expressed in Documents 69 and 70.

The mingling of political, economic, and religious matters is presented in Documents 71 and 72. The first is included in this period, rather than in Part II, because it has more relevance. The second selection, from the King, indicates an awareness of Frontenac's behaviour. The last letter is Frontenac's justification of his activities. Within two years he was recalled.

*63. "PROVISIONS OF GOVERNOR AND LIEUTENANT-GENERAL IN CANADA, ACADIA, . . . NEWFOUDLAND AND OTHER LANDS OF FRANCE IN THE NORTH FOR . . . FRONTENAC, VERSAILLES, APRIL 7, 1672" (*Ordonnances et Jugements*, Vol. 3, pp. 40-42).

* * *

We have resolved to recall the Sieur de Courcelle from the post of Governor and Lieutenant-General of Canada and to establish in his place a person of qualities and fidelity in whom we can confide the conduct of our peoples of the said country, the care of the increase of Christianity, the amelioration of commerce, and the growth of the colonies. . . . We have . . . to this end, chosen our dearly beloved . . . Sieur Comte de Frontenac who has given many proofs of his experience and worth and we know him to have all the qualities necessary to fulfil with dignity the said duties.

For these reasons . . . the said . . . Sieur de Frontenac . . . is established by these present, signed by our hand, Governor and Lieutenant-General . . . to have command of all governors and our lieutenants established in the said countries, as well as the officials of the Sovereign Council which is established, and over French vessels . . . of war belonging to us or merchant ships . . . .

We enjoin the said . . . officials . . . and others to acknowledge . . . Frontenac, and to obey him in all that he orders them. He will assemble the estates, when necessary, to take up arms. He will take cognizance of, reconciliate and accommodate all differences that exist or may exist in the said country be it between the seigniors and the principals or between individual inhabitants. He will establish garrisons where needed. Command, as well the people of the . . . countries, as all our other subjects, cleric, noble, or men of war . . . .

LOUIS

COLBERT

Registered in the records of the Sovereign Council . . . at Quebec, . . . September 12, 1672.

*64. ". . . MINISTER TO FRONTENAC, JUNE 13, 1673"
(*R.A.P.Q.*, 1926-27, pp. 24-26).

. . . I will repeat again to you that His Majesty has not planned on giving any assistance to Canada this year because of the large and prodigious expenses that he has been obliged to make for the raising of . . . 200,000 soldiers presently mobilized . . . and one hundred ships and twenty-five galleys presently at sea. He has not neglected to again incur the expenses for the sending of sixty young women and has given some assistance to the hospital at Quebec and to a few individuals, but this is all he was capable of doing for this year . . . .

65. "EXTRACT FROM THE LETTER OF FATHER NOUVEL . . . WRITTEN FROM STE. MARIE DU SAULT TO . . . THE GOVERNOR, MAY 29, 1673" (Thwaites, *Jesuit Relations*, Vol. 57, pp. 21-23).

As it is important that you be informed of all notable occurrences in these parts, here is a faithful narrative of them.

The Savages among whom we live have never appeared to us more disposed to embrace Christianity than at present, because of the good treatment that they received last year from Monsieur de Courcelle and the attentions of all the French with whom they live. Their trade has done much towards this, and the continuation of it is very important. We try as much as we can, conformable to what . . . the Governor and . . . Intendant have written to us about it, to incline them to continue their intercourse with the French. But already we see that the establishment of the English on the great bay of the North, and the proximity of the Iroquois, with whom the missisakis have pursued their winter hunting, will cause a decided prejudice against the colony. The English have already diverted a great many of the inland savages who visit lake Superior, and attracted them to themselves by their great liberality; and the Iroquois have sent very considerable presents to all the nations to confirm, they say, the Peace that Onnontio made — but rather to get their peltries, with which the Iroquois are expecting these tribes to respond to their presents. Some of the Savages of these regions, who saw during the winter the Savages from the interior who made their trade last autumn with des groisiliers and the English, have assured us that two ships had arrived at that great bay, and that they were annoyed by a third, which followed them, and from which they apprehend shipwreck. They added that about two hundred men were put ashore, and that in four days they had erected a large house, which they fortified with several pieces of cannon. The savages greatly praised their liberality. I learned yesterday that they are to hold a great council with all the neighbouring nations around them. All these tidings trouble the savages attached to us, who are enjoying the peace that the victorious arms of the King have acquired for them; they have some fears lest all this be disturbed by these revolutions. We do not fail, thereupon, to give them the necessary encouragement to keep themselves closely united both with God and with the French, assuring them that in this union they have no reason to fear.

* * *

*66. "FRONTENAC TO COLBERT, QUEBEC, NOVEMBER 13, 1673" (*R.A.P.Q.*, 1926-27, pp. 26-52).

* * *

I was advised . . . by . . . Lasalle who was with the Iroquois and by the Jesuit Fathers . . . that the English, by underhand means, were doing what they could to convince the Ottawas to sign a treaty and break their peace with us, representing to them that a more favourable moment would not come again as Canada was without troops and had a new governor who had, as yet, little knowledge or experience . . . .

*   *   *

I immediately dispatched . . . Lasalle to the Iroquois with presents for them, as is the custom . . . .

I also made provisions, as secretly as possible, of all that I considered necessary for the establishment of the post* . . . and construction of the fort, and made arrangements to meet in Montreal by June 1 . . . .

*   *   *

This enterprise was very successful being accomplished in very little time and without the loss of a single man or canoe . . . which here is considered miraculous.

But, Monseigneur, the approbation here is nothing if I do not have yours as well, for my unique goal was to be of service to the King . . . .

I hope, as well, that you will find the costs low, as you may see from the statement I send . . . .

*   *   *

I made all the necessary advances from my own pocket and on my credit except those materials drawn from the King's stores . . . for I will never spare myself and will do all in my power for the King's service, and I hope, if you think it fit, that you will reimburse me from the funds available here.

I will even furnish all the merchandise necessary for the coming winter and spring, and without which one could not attract the Indians, until such time as you advise me of your approval of a company which I have proposed be formed by some of the principal merchants of the country for the maintenance of the post.

FRONTENAC

*   *   *

67. "MEMOIR FOR THE MAINTENANCE OF FORT FRONTENAC, 1674" (O'Callaghan, *Colonial History of the State of New York*, Vol. 9, p. 122).

The proposer, aware of the importance to the Colony of Canada of the establishment of Fort Frontenac, of which he was some time in command, and desiring to employ his means and his life in the King's service and for the augmentation of the Country, offers to support it at his expense, and to reimburse its cost on the following conditions, to wit:

---

* Fort Frontenac, now Kingston, Ontario.

That his Majesty be pleased to grant in seigniory to the proposer the said fort, four leagues of country along the border of Lake Frontenac, the two Islands in front . . . and the interjacent Islets, with the same rights and privileges obtained hitherto by those who hold lands in the country in seigniory . . . together with the command of the said place . . . under the orders and authority of his Majesty's Governor, . . . on which conditions the proposer will be bound:

1st. To maintain the said fort; to place it in a better state of defense; to keep a garrison there at least as numerous as that of Montreal, and as many as fifteen to twenty labourers during the first two years to clear and till the land; to provide it with necessary artillery, arms, and ammunition . . . .

2d. To repay Count de Frontenac . . . the expenses he incurred for the establishment of the said Fort, amounting to the sum of twelve to thirteen thousand livres . . . .

3d. To make grants of land to all those willing to settle there . . . .

4th. To attract thither the greatest possible number of Indians . . . .

5th. To build a Church when there will be one hundred persons, meanwhile to entertain from this moment one of two Recollet friars . . . .

DE LA SALLE

*   *   *

*68. "INFORMATION AND DECLARATIONS ON THE SUBJECT OF A SERMON BY THE SIEUR ABBÉ DE FÉNELON ON EASTER DAY, MARCH 25, 1674 IN THE PARISH CHURCH OF MONTREAL, MAY 2, 1674" (*R.A.P.Q.*, 1921-22, pp. 129-33).

*   *   *

René Robert Cavelier, Sieur de la Salle . . .

Deposes that the Sieur de Fénelon preaching on Easter day in the Church of Montreal at high mass used as the topic of his sermon that we ought to imitate the death of Christ and partake of his resurrection . . . .

After casually noting the effects of this resurrection on the people of all estates he spoke of those in authority in approximately these words: that he who has authority should not trouble the people dependent upon him but rather that he should consider them as his children and treat them as would a father; that he should not disturb the commerce of the country by maltreating those who do not share the profits with him; that he should gain his ends by legal means; that he should not trample people nor burden them with extraordinary corvées that profit but himself; that he should not create favourites who praise but himself not should he oppress those who serve the same ruler when they expose his enterprises . . . .

These statements and others . . . appear to be directed to . . . Monseigneur the Count de Frontenac, governor . . . in this country . . . .

*69. "MINISTER TO FRONTENAC, JUNE 13, 1673"
(*R.A.P.Q.*, 1926-27, pp. 24-26).

*   *   *

The assembly, and division of all the inhabitants of the country which you called in order that they might swear allegiance may have produced a good effect at the time but it is well that you note that you must always follow in the government and conduct of that country the forms used here. The King has not, for a long time, called together the Estates General believing this to be beneficial to his service. . . . In order to slowly abolish this ancient form you should rarely, to be more accurate, never, use this form and, when the colony is better established, you should suppress the syndic who presents requests in the name of all the people, for it is well that each speak for himself and none for all.

*   *   *

*70. "COLBERT TO FRONTENAC, MAY 17, 1674"
(*R.A.P.Q.*, 1926-27, pp. 55-60).

I have reported to the King the contents of your letter of November 13 last . . . and His Majesty has heard the details with satisfaction and requested that I explain his intentions on the contents . . . .

*   *   *

As to the regulations concerning general policy which you have made, and the establishment of aldermen to whom you have granted judicial powers, His Majesty orders me to inform you that you have exceeded the powers he granted you . . . in that general policy must be legislated by the Sovereign Council over which you preside, and not on your own authority . . . .

*   *   *

You will easily recognize from what I have . . . said, and more so in the light of the state of affairs in Europe which I explained at the beginning of this letter, that it is not His Majesty's intention that you make distant voyages nor that the inhabitants should extend themselves. To the contrary, he desires that you work assiduously, and at all times, . . . at gathering the inhabitants into cities and villages . . . .

This general rule may have two exceptions: on the one hand, if the country of which you take possession is necessary for commerce and trade . . . .

The other exception being the possession of a country which would shorten communications with France . . . .

* * *

His Majesty orders me to recommend to you the person and interests of the Sieur Perrot, governor of Montreal and nephew of Talon . . . .

*71. "DIRECTIVE EXCOMMUNICATING THOSE WHO SELL INTOXI-
CATING LIQUORS TO THE INDIANS, QUEBEC, MAY 5, 1660"
(Mandements des Évêques, Vol. 1, pp. 14-15).*

. . . François de Laval, by the grace of God and the Holy See, Bishop of Petraea, Apostolic Vicar . . . of New France and adjacent countries . . .

Being aware of the great disorders caused in the past by intoxicating wines and spirits given to the Indians and the more deadly consequences . . . ; Seeing also the orders of the King expressly prohibiting all inhabitants of this country, merchants, factors, captains, sailors, passengers, and all other, from dealing, in any way, in wines or spirits with the Indians, on pain of corporal punishment; Seeing further the regulations of the Governors . . . to stop these disorders . . . notwithstanding which the evil increases day by day, which excesses are not only a public scandal but also imperil Christianity [and] the fear we have that a justly irritated God may withdraw his grace from us and the dire punishments which may befall this Church which it has pleased his Divince Grace to entrust to our care though we are unworthy of it. Finally, obliged to bring extreme measures to bear on these evils we, to this effect, expressly prohibit . . . on pain of excommunication incurred *ipso facto*, to give in payment to the Indians, sell, trade or give gratuitously . . . either wine or spirits in any form or fashion or on any pretext whatsoever, reserving to ourselves the absolution of the said excommunications. We declare, however, that these prohibitions . . . do not include the few cases, which seldom occur, when one cannot help but give a little of these spirits as might be the case in long, fatiguing and extraordinary voyages and similar necessities. But even in these cases, excommunication will be incurred if the said portion exceeds the usual portions which person of conscience and probity are accustomed to serve to domestics in this country. And all those who use this as a pretext to commit fraud and deceit . . . will remember that nothing is hidden from God and that deceiving men will not stop the malediction and just anger of God from falling upon them . . . .

FRANÇOIS . . .

*72 "THE KING TO FRONTENAC, ST. GERMAIN, APRIL 29, 1680"
(*R.A.P.Q.*, 1926-27, pp. 113-16).

*   *   *

As to the matter of the coureur de bois, what is going on is entirely
contrary to the orders which I have given you . . . and I cannot accept the
excuse you allege . . . that it is the intendant who authorizes the coureur
de bois because of the commerce in which he is engaged . . . it is clear to
me that the fault lies with you as you favour those engaged in the trade
which is totally contrary to the well-being . . . of the . . . colony . . . .

*73. "FRONTENAC TO THE MARÉCHAL DE BELLEFONDS, QUEBEC,
NOVEMBER 14, 1680" (*R.A.P.Q.*, 1926-27, pp. 117-18).

*   *   *

You know, Monseigneur, better than anyone, what happens when one
is involved and close to events which others, being distant, see otherwise
because of the distortions used to mislead.

In spite of the prejudices that M. Colbert may have with regards to my
diligence, and the part I have played in the divisions of this country, I
do not despair that he will soon be disabused and others than myself
will let him know that I have the least contributed to the troubles.

*   *   *

Thus I will suffer all, I will complain against no one and will remain
. . . inactive except in the matter of the coureur de bois . . . following the
orders which I am given . . . .

But after doing all that is possible it is not just that M. Colbert blame
me for the bad consequences of the revocation of the trade permits . . .
as I had always foreseen them . . . .

                                                FRONTENAC

B

THE CANADIAN CHURCH

Before 1663 the Catholic Church of New France was organized to serve the needs of missionary endeavours among the Indians. The administrative structures were highly centralized with all authority radiating from the head of the mission at Quebec, and in 1659, from the new Bishop. The material needs of the missions were met by contributions from the devout and the resources of the Jesuit order. The spiritual needs of the small French population were also served, but as a secondary function.

The introduction of Royal Government radically changed the position of the Church in Canada. Its dominant position within the society was challenged by the State and it was finally subordinated to the royal will. The Canadian Church was decidedly Gallican.

The rapid increase of the population shifted the primary concern of the Church from missionary work to the servicing of the secular and spiritual needs of the Canadian populace. Many more priests, churches, and schools were needed. The result was a reorganization of the Church in Canada along lines similar to those of the political and economic structures of the society.

Payment of the tithe was incumbent upon all Catholics. In Documents 74 and 75 we see the tithe established and quickly reduced and restricted in its application. No doubt poverty among the inhabitants was one valid reason for this; however, there is some significance in the fact that the tithe was never applied to the most remunerative commercial occupation of the Canadians: the fur trade.

In prior documents we have seen that the authority of the Church extended over the material interests of the laity. The determination of the proper forms of salutation or the excommunication of those who traded liquor for furs resulted in conflicts. Document 76 illustrates another such conflict, and, as was usual in New France, the ultimate arbiter was the State.

Differences between members of the same State, however, did not extend to matters of faith. The co-operation of the intendant evidenced in Document 77 was the rule. The moral pleas of Laval, and his successor as Bishop, St.-Vallier, were to some extent adhered to. No one disputed the rights of the Bishop to dominance in the domain of ethics, although the repeated admonitions of the Bishop, Documents 80 to 82, suggest that the *Canadiens* misbehaved at times.

In education, the Church occupied the role that the state fulfils today. The educational accomplishments of the Canadian Church in New France were significant. The establishment of the Seminary of Quebec by Laval provided a Canadian institution for the education of future clerics. The Jesuit College, as well as the schools of the Ursulines, the Congrégation de Notre Dame, and the Sulpicians, were the public and high schools of their day. Another facet of the Church's work in education is evident in Document 79: the incorporation, through education, of the Indians into Canadian society.

The efforts of the Church and State to establish parishes is recounted in Document 80. Again we see secular resistance to the Church. At the same time the material difficulties of erecting parishes, because a colonial society was too poor to support a complex religious structure, are presented.

*74. "DECLARATION CONCERNING THE TITHE, QUEBEC, FEBRUARY 1, 1664" (*Mandements des Évêques*, Vol. 1, pp. 160-61).

To All Inhabitants, Greetings.

Having had registered in the records of the Sovereign Council the establishment of the tithes following the Decree of the King dated April 1663 by which they were established at $\frac{1}{13}$; and having declared, because of the present state of the country, that they would be assessed at $\frac{1}{20}$ for six years, . . . nevertheless there have been difficulties in their payment. Wishing to show our affection for the inhabitants we offered to have the tithes continued at $\frac{1}{20}$ for our lifetime which, still not being pleasing, we voluntarily consent to await the return of the vessels of the year 1665 so that they may present to His Majesty the reasons for their objections. In the meantime we have taken the resolution to serve the inhabitants gratuitously according to our abilities and resources . . . .

FRANÇOIS . . .

*   *   *

*75. "DECLARATION CONCERNING THE TITHE, QUEBEC, MARCH 10, 1664" (*Mandements des Évêques*, Vol. 1, p. 161).

You will be advised that a few persons, having misunderstood a word that is in the act establishing the tithes, have sown in the spirit of the people false ideas and calumnies, saying that we wished to exact the tithe on eggs, cabbages, planks, cords of wood, and generally all manufactured products, which is contrary to the facts, contrary to universal custom, and contrary to the intention of the Church. For the word labour of men, which is mentioned in the act, means but the cultivation of the soil.

FRANÇOIS . . .

*   *   *

*76. "DECREE OF THE SUPERIOR COUNCIL RE THE TITHE . . .
QUEBEC, NOVEMBER 18, 1705" (*Arrêts et Règlements*, Vol.
2, pp. 133-35).

. . . The King's Attorney-General has been advised . . . that the parish
priests . . . of l'Ange-Gardien . . . and of Beauport have, from their pul-
pits, last Sunday and on preceding Sundays, informed their parishioners
that, notwithstanding their having paid their tithes on grains only, as
has been the practice in the past, they must now pay the tithe on all
products of the soil, . . . domestic animals, . . . fruits, hemp, sheep, and
other produce, which caused much murmuring amongst the inhabitants
after the mass . . . .

* * *

This being so, it is necessary to note that . . . de Tracy, Courcelle, and
Talon, . . . in 1665 . . . came to an agreement with . . . Laval . . . whom
His Majesty had named as first Bishop of the country . . . providing that
the tithe, in the future, would be exacted on grains only, at the rate of
$\frac{1}{26}$ . . . payable at the presbytery.

The Council . . . orders . . . that the said parish priests shall appear
in person before it to justify the authority for their claims . . . .

RAUDOT [INTENDANT]

*77. "TALON TO COLBERT, QUEBEC, OCTOBER 7, 1665"
(*R.A.P.Q.*, 1930-31, p. 39).

Since my last dispatch we . . . de Tracy, de Courcelle, and myself, have
assisted at the abjuration of M. Bernier, captain in the Carignan Salières
regiment, of his heresy to . . . the Bishop of Petraea. . . . Since my arrival
less than a month ago this is the sixteenth conversion. . . . As I know that
this officer embraced the religion of Your Majesty in spite of the ruin of
his domestic and family affairs, I am persuaded that he will have difficulties subsisting unless Your Majesty has the goodness to grant him a
boon as he has no hope of assistance from his parents.

TALON

*78. "ASSENT OF THE KING TO THE ESTABLISHMENT OF THE
SEMINARY OF QUEBEC . . . APRIL, 1667"
(*Édits, Ordonnances Royaux*, Vol. 1, pp. 35-36).

After having examined in our councils the act of establishment and erection of the said seminary we believe that nothing could be more advantageous to the greater glory of God and the well-being of our subjects . . . [and we] ordain . . . that the tithe . . . will be destined forever . . . to the foundation and maintenance of the seminary and its clergy . . . .

LOUIS

79. "DUCHESNEAU TO SEIGNELAY, NOVEMBER 13, 1681" (O'Callaghan, *Colonial History of the State of New York*, Vol. 9, p. 150).

. . . at the mission of the Mountain of Montreal governed by the gentlemen of the Seminary of Saint Sulpice, and in that of the Sault of la Prairie de la Madeleine, in its vicinity; and those of Sillery and Loretto in the neighbourhood of Quebec, all three under the direction of the Jesuit Fathers, the youth are all brought up 'à la française' except in the manner of their food and dress, which it is necessary to make them retain in order that they be not effeminate, and that they be more at liberty and less impeded whilst hunting, which constitutes their wealth and ours.

A commencement has been made in all these missions to instruct the young boys in reading and writing; at that of the Montreal Mountain, the Ladies of the Congregation devote themselves to the instruction of the little girls, and employ them in needlework; the Ursulines at Quebec act in the same way towards those given to them, whom they receive indifferently from all the missions, whether established among us or in the Indian Country under the direction of the Jesuit Fathers.

On this point, My Lord you will permit me, if you please, to state two things to you. First, those missions cannot be too much encouraged, nor too much countenance be given to the gentlemen of Saint Sulpice and the Jesuit Fathers among the Indians, inasmuch as they not only place the Country in security and bring peltries hither, but greatly glorify God, and the King, as eldest son of the Church, by reason of the large number of good Christians formed here.

Secondly, his Majesty may, perhaps have it in his power to increase essentially this great good, were he to order me to make, in his name, a few presents to the Indians of the Villages established among us, so as to attract a greater number of them; and were he to destine a small fund for the Indian girls who quit the Ursulines, on being educated, to fit them out and marry them, and establish Christian families through their means.

*   *   *

80. "DUCHESNEAU TO SEIGNELAY, NOVEMBER 13, 1681"
     (O'Callaghan, *Colonial History of the State of New
     York*, Vol. 9, pp. 150-51).

*   *   *

You will perceive, My Lord, by the letter I have written to the proprietors of lands in justice and in fief, as well for themselves as for their
settlers, that after having conferred with the Bishop, as you ordered me
to do in everything regarding the spiritualities of this Country, and in
obedience to the King's intentions and to yours, the tythe alone is to
constitute the support of a Parish Priest who has been furnished with a
district supposed to be large enough for that purpose and even the
extent of this has been submitted to the decision of the proprietors and
settlers, in order that if by them considered too large it should be
curtailed, and likewise, if not sufficiently large, it should be increased.

Nevertheless, My Lord, the proprietors of the fiefs and the seigniories,
and the settlers have represented that by increasing the extent of the
Parish the people would have been rendered more destitute, because, as
heretofore laid out . . . the settlers constituting it had mass usually but
one Sunday in a month or six weeks; that the tythe even would not
increase in consequence of adding to the Missions, because the settlers
being visited more rarely, would declare against paying tythe except in
proportion to the attendance they might receive . . . .

The parish priests have, on the other hand, represented that they are
already surcharged with work, being obliged to be incessantly travelling,
now on snow shoes over the snows in winter, and anon during the summer in a canoe, which they paddle the whole day long; and that if their
Missions, already too extensive, be enlarged, they would not be able to
stand such excessive fatigue.

*   *   *

. . . My Lord, I must inform you that there is not a single person in
this country who is capable of endowing a Church with 111 lb.,* but is
able even to build it substantially at his own expense. Everybody here
is puffed up with the greatest vanity; there is not one but pretends to be
a patron, and wants a Curé on his farm; and all these persons are steeped
in debt, and in the extremest poverty, with one exception, and he is the
poorer because he is a sordid miser.

*81. ". . . AGAINST LUXURY AND VANITY OF WOMEN AND GIRLS IN
     CHURCH, QUEBEC, FEBRUARY 26, 1682" (*Mandements des
     Évêques*, Vol. 1, pp. 106-8).

---

* A poor translation of *livre*, a unit of French money. See appendix F.

If the Fathers and Doctors of the Church censure with force against the luxury and vanity of girls and women who, forgetting the promises of their baptism, appear dressed and ornamented with displays of Satan which they so solemnly renounced, it is to indicate to us the extreme horror that God has of such a disorder, which makes those who are guilty of it all the more guilty before Him, in that, wishing to please the eyes of men, they make themselves the captives and instruments of the Demon who uses this luxury to make them, and those who see them, commit an infinity of sins. . . . If these vain appearances displease God so strongly, . . . of what crime are they not guilty, and what punishment might be expected by those who wear this ostentatious apparel . . . in our churches, appearing in these consecrated places to pray and do penance in indecent apparel, showing a scandalous nudity of arms, shoulders, and throats, contenting themselves with covering them with a transparent fabric which only serves to give lustre to these shameful nudities; the head bared or but covered with a transparent net and the hair curled in a manner unworthy of a Christian person . . . .

For these causes we expressly prohibit all women and girls of no matter what rank or consideration to approach the sacraments . . . in the indecent manners specified . . . .

FRANÇOIS

*82. "ADVICE GIVEN TO THE GOVERNOR AND HIS WIFE ON THE OBLIGATIONS THEY HAVE TO SET A GOOD EXAMPLE FOR THE POPULATION, 1685-1686(?)" (*Mandements des Évêques,* Vol. 1, pp. 169-74).

* * *

ON FEASTS

1) When . . . the Governor and his wife invite people to eat with them it is proper that it be for dinner rather than for supper and in so doing, avoid entertaining them during an extended evening and avoid dangerous pastimes and other vexatious habits which arise at banquets and night assemblies.

2) They should declare themselves unhappy, be uncivil, and even dismiss for ever their guests, should the meal which is given to them be too sumptuous and magnificient. In this way, finding themselves at meals that are frugal, they will accustom, bit by bit, their guests to the avoidance of too sumptuous feasts which are not only inconvenient . . . but opposed to temperance and wound Christian modesty and decorum.

3) They should never suffer these feasts to be accompanied by dances or balls, and several other dangerous and licentious recreations. Their presence at these divertissements would cause great harm as past experience has shown . . . .

ON BALLS AND DANCES

While balls and dances, in themselves, are harmless by nature, nevertheless they are dangerous because of the environment they provide, and the evil, and almost inevitable consequences that follow . . . it is best not to find oneself at balls or dances unless one is absolutely obliged, in which cases they should season these divertissements with great modesty, good intentions, dignity, and Christian consideration and pious sentiments, so that one may preserve oneself from corruption . . . .

* * *

As the age and vivacity of their daughter necessitates a few diversions and recreations one may deign to permit her a few honest and moderate dances but with people of her own sex only and in the presence of . . . her mother for fear that none too decent words and songs are used, and never in the presence of men and boys, for this mixing of sexes, frankly speaking, is the cause of the inconveniences and disorders of balls and dances . . . .

ON COMEDIES AND OTHER PLAYS

. . . We do not believe that Christian decorum permits the representation of comedies, or to appear before an audience as an actress declaiming verses, no matter how holy the subject matter. And less still should we suffer that boys declaim with girls . . . .

JEAN

* * *

*83. "ORODNNANCE OBLIGING INHABITANTS TO BE RESPECTFUL IN CHURCHES AND PROHIBITING THEM FROM QUARRELLING . . . AND LEAVING THE CHURCH DURING THE SERMON, NOVEMBER 12, 1706" (*Arrêts et Règlements,* Vol. 2, p. 425).

. . . Gauthier, the parish priest of . . . Beaupré, seeing with sorrow . . . many disorders amongst his parishioners . . . indicating a lack of respect due to God . . . and specifically . . . two inhabitants . . . who were drunk during the service . . . and other parishioners . . . that leave the church during the sermon to smoke . . .

And being persuaded that these disorders are due to the ease with which liquor may be purchased on . . . Sunday . . .

. . . We prohibit . . . on any pretext . . . the sale of liquor . . . on Sundays . . . .

And . . . everyone is also prohibited from quarelling . . . or talking in Churches; from leaving during the sermon and from smoking at the church door or about the church.

* * *

RAUDOT

C

THE ECONOMY OF NEW FRANCE

One of the aims of the French State was to establish a viable and diversified economy in New France. The instructions to Gaudais in 1663, and those of Talon in 1665, envisioned a colony that was not merely self-sufficient, but capable of exporting her products, agricultural and industrial, to France and the West Indies. These plans and visions came to little. Talon did establish a few industries, such as shipbuilding and a brewery, but lack of population, markets, skilled workmen, capital, and, most important, support from France, led to a continued dependence on the fur staple.

The search for furs, as has been noted, was a factor in Champlain's choice of Quebec as the site for a permanent colony. The mystic realization that was Montreal rapidly gave way to the economic exploitation of the locale as a centre of commerce. Frontenac's westward push to Lake Ontario, and LaSalle's southward orientation are also part of the continentalism so evident in the French Régime. Furs were not merely the staple of the economy but the catalyst of the political, military, and social elements in the colony. Documents 84 to 92 trace the impact of the fur trade on these elements in Canadian society.

The recall of Frontenac in 1682 did not mark the end of his influence. Documents 83 and 84 are concerned with the results of his policies of expansion, and a criticism of the favouritism of the new governor, La Barre.

The following five selections consider the economic activities of the secular aristocracy. In New France nobles were permitted to trade. The loss of noble status for engaging in commerce, which is called *dérogeance*, was mandatory in Old France but not in the New. The results of the privileged position of the Canadian noble were that the landed, administrative, military, and commercial élites of Canada formed a compact, influential, and often vociferous group capable of exercising power at all levels.

The Compagnie du Nord was a Canadian enterprise directed against the English establishments on the Hudson's Bay. Document 89 presents the terms of incorporation, and the following selection illustrates the use by the Canadians of the diplomatic power of France. The purely military aspects of the endeavour will be presented in Section E: War.

The extensive readings on the Company of Canada indicate the means and ends of a new Canadian company. For the first time since the days of Frontenac, the Canadians presented a united front. The new company included the Compagnie du Nord and every important fur trader in Canada. The North, West, and South arms of the fur trade were united under one Canadian-financed and -administered monopoly.

The creation of a Canadian monetary system is the subject-matter of Documents 93 and 94. The cards used by the intendant were the equivalent of a post-dated cheque or a promissory note. Their value depended upon public confidence and the ability of the Royal treasury to redeem them.

The selection on foreign commerce in Canada (Document 95) illustrates the mixture of economics, politics, and war. Both France and New France were expected to benefit from the trade embargoes placed on foreigners.

Land was the second great economic asset of New France. The Crown used the seigniorial system to reward its servants, and to populate the country. Large grants of land were given to individuals at minimal costs and obligations. In return the recipient, the seignior, undertook to develop the land and establish settlers at his own expense. The system, on the whole, produced the desired results, but was also subject to some abuse by the secular aristocracy. The responsibility for the implementation of the system lay with the intendant. The efforts of one intendant, Raudot, are presented in Document 96. The Crown's remedy of the ills of the system are contained in the Edicts of Marly, Document 97. There were two Edicts, one directed against abuses by the seigniors, and the second was meant to apply against the *censitaire* who failed to fulfil his obligations. The first was not applied for over 30 years. The second Edict was applied immediately.

*84. "PROPOSAL TO ATTACK THE IROQUOIS, OCTOBER 10, 1682" (O'Callaghan, *Documentary History of the State of New York*, Vol. 1, pp. 96-99).

At a meeting held the tenth of October 1682, composed of M. the Governor, M. the Intendant, M. the Bishop of Quebec, M. Dollier, Superior of the Seminary of St. Sulpice at Montreal, the Rev. Fathers Beschefer, Superior, D'Ablon and Fremin, Jesuits, M. the Major of the City, Messrs. de Varenne, Governor of Three Rivers, de Brussy, Dalibout,

Duquet, Lemoine, Ladutantais, Bizard, Vieuxpont, Duluth, de Sorel, Derepentigny, Berthier, and Boucher.

It is proposed by M. the Governor, that from records which M. the Count de Frontenac was pleased to deposit in his hands of what had passed at Montreal on the 12 Sept. last, between him and the Deputy of the Onontague Iroquois, it is easy to infer that these people are inclined to follow the object of their enterprise, which is to destroy all the Nations in alliance with us, . . . whilst they keep us in uncertainty and with folded arms; so that, after having deprived us of the entire fur trade which they wish alone to carry on with the English and Dutch established at Manate and Orange, they may attack us isolated, and ruin the colony in obliging it to contract itself and abandon all the separate settlements, and thus arrest the cultivation . . . .

85. "MEMOIR TO THE GENTLEMEN PARTNERS OF THE SOCIETY INVESTED WITH THE FARM AND COMMERCE OF CANADA, ON WAYS TO PREVENT FRAUDS IN BEAVERS" (Preston and Lamontagne, *Royal Fort Frontenac*, pp. 131-32).

*   *   *

. . . The said beavers can be prevented from falling into the hands of the said farmers by several places of which the first is Katarakouy or Fort Frontenac. This post is situated on the edge of Lake Ontario. It was established in the year 1673 by M. the Count Frontenac, purportedly for the security of the country, but in fact for trading with the Iroquois, to serve as a refuge and "entrepôt" for the "Coureurs de bois" scattered among all the Ottawa nations, and to form a trading connection in beavers with the Dutch and the English of Albany and Manhattan.

*   *   *

Monsieur de la Barre who has succeeded the said Count Frontenac in the government of Canada thought this post necessary for the success of the continual enterprises of Sieur de la Chenaye who has sent there a large consignment of goods in the care of Sergeant Champagne on the pretext of supplying and protecting the said fort, which is said to have been abandoned by the said Sieur de la Salle . . . .

*86. "PERMISSION GIVEN TO NOBLES TO TRADE, AUGUST 25, 1685" (*Jugements et Déliberations*, Vol. 2, p. 1019).

. . . Registration of the judgment . . . of the King . . . of last March . . . by which his Majesty permits the nobles and gentlemen established in this country to engage in commerce on land and sea . . . .

DE MEULLES [INTENDANT]

*87. "MEMOIR TO MONSEIGNEUR DE SEIGNELAY ON THE AFFAIRS
OF THE BAY OF THE NORTH IN CANADA, QUEBEC,
OCTOBER 12, 1712" (*R.A.P.Q.*, 1947-1948, pp. 189-90).

The French did not oppose the introduction of the English in the Bay
by . . . Desgrozeliers and Radisson because, for several years, they had no
knowledge of this enterprise. But as soon as they knew of it they sent
memoirs to . . . Colbert on the importance of this usurpation and of the
necessity of removing . . . the English. . . . However, the good relations
existing at the time between the King and His Britannic Majesty led to
no action been taken. . . . Colbert contented himself with writing to
Duchesneau . . . that it would be advantageous to the King's service to
go to the Hudson's Bay to contest the proprietary right of the English . . .
as the lands fell within the domain of the French Crown. . . . The Colony
of Canada increasing bit by bit in population and multiplying day by
day, considered the usurpation by the English of the Bay threatened the
total ruin of their commerce, this . . . led in 1682 to the formation of a
company . . . to sustain their commerce in . . . the Bay of the North.

COLLATED BY VAUDREUIL [GOVERNOR]
BÉGON [INTENDANT]

*88. "CHARLEVOIX ON THE HUDSON'S BAY" (Charlevoix, *Histoire
de la Nouvelle France,* Vol. 3, pp. 306-7).

*   *   *

The capture of Fort Bourbon, although it would have assured for a
long time to the French the possession of all of the North of Canada, did
not recompense the King for the expenses undertaken in . . . America
for that year . . . However, the commerce of the Hudson's Bay was much
more considerable than most people thought and we have seen the consequences. . . . What is certain is that the pelts of the Bay are much
better than any others and that the extreme indigence of the Indians of
that country is the reason that they may be had at a very good price.

*89. "COMPAGNIE DU NORD, OCTOBER 29, 1685"
(*Jugements et Délibérations,* Vol. 2, pp. 1037-38).

Registration by the Council of the judgment of the King's Council . . . of May 20 last . . . in which his Majesty accords and concedes to members of the Compagnie du Nord . . . the Bourbon River and the lands . . . along its shores for a fur-trading establishment, and the construction of forts, habitations, and counters necessary for their commerce, for a period of twenty years. . . . His Majesty also permits the said members to establish two counters at the Abitibi Lakes, and one at Lake Nemiscou. They may trade in the said areas, and for the said time, to the exclusion of all others on condition that they bring to the counters of this city all furs . . . in order to pay, in the accustomed manner, the sums due the King's Domain . . . .

ROUER DE VILLERAY*

*90. "MEMOIR ON THE AFFAIRS OF NORTHERN AMERICA PRE-
SENTED TO HIS BRITANNIC MAJESTY BY . . . DE BARILLON
AND DE BONREPAUS,† OCTOBER 1687" (P.A.C., M.G. 1,
Series 3, Vol. 11, pp. 279-89).

*   *   *

. . . Without going into long details . . . we would inform your Majesty that the English Company have claimed in their memorandums:

1 — That the French Company has caused it great losses . . . for which they claim damages.

2 — That the property of the Hudson's Bay belongs to them, and presented several narratives proving the priority of their claims.

4 — That a patent of the year 1670 permits and concedes to them the commerce of the said Bay.

To which the French Company answered:

2 — . . . Rather than mere narratives and other things advanced by the English with regards to priority of possession, the French produced original acts and titles in due form proving that as early as the year 1523 these lands had been discovered by orders of the King of France; that in the year 1540 the Sieur de Roberval took possession of them . . . and that in the year 1598 King Henry the Great issued a similar commission to the Sieur de la Roches. . . . In 1628 . . . Louis XIII established a new company to which he conceded all the countries of Canada . . . .

4 — As to the patent of the year 1670 which conceded the commerce of the Bay to the English Company, the French respond that this patent could not be conceded to the prejudice of that of Louis XIII of the year 1628 . . . .

. . . Before the year 1668 or 1669 the English had no establishment in

---

* First councillor in the Sovereign Council of New France.

† De Barillon and de Bonrepaus represented the French Crown in negotiations with the Court of St. James re ownership of the Hudson's Bay.

the Hudson's Bay, nor any knowledge of the commerce that might be engaged in, and that . . . Desgroselliers and Radisson, Frenchmen by birth and employees of the French Company . . . came to London where they informed several merchants . . . that they would indicate to them places where the English might establish themselves without the French knowing of it. . . . These individuals having made a considerable profit from their sale of the peltries, formed a company to which was accorded in 1670 the concession of all we have spoken of above.

91. "BEAVER TRADE AGREEMENT, PARIS, MAY 15, 1700" (P.A.C. *Report*, 1928, pp. 32-41).

Special agreement between thes Colony of Canada and the Farmer of the Western Domain* to reconcile their interests with regard to the consumption of the beaver belonging to them by means of a concentration of the beaver of both parties into one hand, which may re-establish the trade on a good commercial basis both in France and in foreign countries.

*   *   *

4

For which lot of beaver as well as for the Farms of Canada, including the quarter of beaver in kind, and for the hat monopoly of the Kingdom, Guigue had to pay to the King the sum of 200,000 livres a year as rent for the farm; from which the King having had the goodness to grant him a reduction of 30,000 livres a year for the remaining years of his lease, he now pays only 170,000 livres.

5

Besides the beaver of the King's contract Guigue has further received and paid for, with his own money, all the following beaver, . . . to wit

     From Hudson's Bay year 1697 . . .
     id. from M. Desevigny 1698 . . .
     id. from the Iroquois 1698 . . .
     id. from M. Desevigny 1699 . . .
     From Canada 1698 and 1699 . . .   total 157,166 livres

6

Which quantity has cost him the following sums . . . to wit . . . 601,610 livres, 2 sous, 7 deniers . . . .

8

The Colony of Canada which by the Decree of the Council of 9th February last has the liberty of trading its beaver for the future independ-

---

* I.e., Guigue.

ently of the Farmer, represents that to facilitate its trade . . . it would need all the beaver which the farmer has . . . .

9

To hand over to it the whole lot of the King's beaver of 672,918 pounds according to the previous statement . . . together with the farms of Canada and that of the hat monopoly for the Kingdom, . . . the whole for the sum of 70,000 livres a year for the ten years remaining of Guigue's lease . . . the said sum payable every year quarterly and in advance . . . .

11

Guigue will further hand over to the Colony into the hands of the commissioners in Paris the quantity of 157,166 pounds of beaver belonging to him in his own property . . . for the sum of 700,000 livres . . . .

12

Thus Guigue will hand over to the Colony the following beaver, . . . 830,084 lbs. . . .

22

The Colony being obliged to pay in Canada every year according to ordinary custom the expenses of the budget of each year as a deduction from the 170,000 livres the price of the Farm. . . .

25

The colony will ratify the present agreements by a deed authenticated in the presence of the Governor, the Bishop, and the Intendant in the course of the present year . . . .

* * *

Drawn up and agreed at Paris to serve as a draft for the regulation to be made in conformity at Paris this 15th May 1700. Signed Richer de Roddes for Guigue and Pascaud . . . .

*92. "STATUTES FOR THE COMPANY OF CANADA, OCTOBER 15, 1700" (*Edits et Ordonnances Royaux,* Vol. 1, pp. 280-84).

The Colony of New France . . . humbly demonstrated this year by their deputies to . . . de Pontchartrain . . . that the principal commerce of the colony since its establishment has been the beaver trade . . . ;

That this trade . . . had brought great profits and that many persons, to the prejudice of the inhabitants, had used their influence to obtain an exclusive monopoly.

The deputies having demonstrated to his Majesty that the preference shown the monopolists was always detrimental to the well-being of the

colony due to their lack of application in developing a market, and the
considerable reduction in the price paid for pelts . . . His Majesty has
permitted the colonists . . . to sell, traffic, and negotiate . . . in France
and in foreign countries the beaver trade of . . . Canada, the Northern
Bay . . . and other areas of Canada, by his decree of February 9 last . . .
and to form a company of merchants and inhabitants in the said
country . . . .

* * *

1 — . . . all the inhabitants of the country may participate in the
company . . . on acquiring a minimum share value of 50 livres . . . .
3 — . . . to avoid complications those who invest in less than 20
shares . . . that is, 1,000 livres, will not be permitted a voice in the deliberations of the company . . . .
4 — All those who purchase 20 or more shares will have a . . . voice
in the assemblies.
5 — All those who have a deliberative voice in the assemblies may be
elected directors of the company.
6 — Company headquarters will be in Quebec City . . . .
16 — All merchants of Canada . . . engaged in the commerce must
join the company and purchase shares proportionate to the business they
do . . . .
26 — The colony, aware as it is of the necessity for a monopoly of the
beaver trade, has amalgamated to itself the company formed for the exploitation of the trade of the Northern Bay.
30 — . . . foreign merchants, presently in the country, who invest . . .
4,000 livres . . . in the company will enjoy the same privileges as the
inhabitants of the country.

93. "INTRODUCTION OF CARD MONEY, QUEBEC, JUNE 8, 1685"
(Shortt, *Currency*, Vol. 1, pp. 69-71).

* * *

Duly considering His Majesty's lack of funds and the need we have
experienced of money for maintaining and subsisting the troops . . . we,
after having subsisted the said troops from our own resources and through
our credit for the period of four or five months, and considering the
scarcity of money in the country, and the inability of the shopkeepers and
others to lend any at present; and after having considered all the measures that we could take for the maintenance of the troops, we have judged
[it] suitable to have notes issued by us . . . Declaring that all the said
notes shall serve them as ready money, and that we shall hold them good
alike for the soldiers and the people of the colony, when they fall into

their hands, assuring them that they shall be paid from the first funds which His Majesty will surely send us by the vessels of the present year . . . .

DE MEULLES [INTENDANT]

94. "MEMORANDUM ON THE CARDS OF CANADA, QUEBEC, SEP-
TEMBER 30, 1706" (Shortt, *Currency*, Vol. 1, pp. 157-59).

The cards which are issued in Canada serve as money just as coin does in France.

The Kingdom of France derives a certain utility from these cards, since, by this means, the King is not obliged to send funds in coined money for the expenditures which he has the goodness to incur. If it were necessary to send this, it would withdraw from the Kingdom annually 100,000 écus. Consequently this currency leaving the country would render money scarcer. It is true one would not appreciate this disadvantage during the abundance of money, nevertheless it is certain that it would effect a diminution. Moreover, France by this device, not sending coined money, runs no risk as to it either from the sea or from enemies.

If coined money were sent to Canada, it would afterwards leave the country by two avenues, one part would return to France, the other would go to New England to purchase certain merchandise, which may be had cheaper there than from France. The part of this money returning to France would run the risks of the sea and enemies. The vessels may be taken or lost, and consequently the money they carry is lost to France, and there can be no greater injury to the Kingdom than the loss of its money.

The other part of this money being carried to New England for the purchase of merchandise, results in a considerable injury to France by the loss of its coinage and the advantage which it would produce among her enemies.

At present the Kingdom of France runs no risk either from the sea or from her enemies, as regards her money, none being sent to this country. The cards they have there serve as money, and procure bills of exchange in France.

Furthermore, there is no fear that money may be carried to New England, which would be very difficult to prevent if there were any in the colony, there being there as in France persons who to gain something would risk much.

It is even a matter of policy for kings to attach the prosperity of their subjects to their own persons, in order to render the former more submissive and to take care that all the means which the colonies may have in money are always in the kingdom on which they are dependent. Canada, having nothing but cards, which are secured only on the word of the King, and seeing no other resource except in the good faith of the sovereign, will be still more submissive to him and still more attached to France for the reason that all the supply it can have in money depends on it. Hence, it appears to me that one cannot do better than to permit the continuation of the card money in Canada.

There may arise great abuses regarding these cards, they may be counterfeited in the country; this, however, can be prevented by a close attention, the easier bestowed as the resources of every person are known. Counterfeits may also be sent from France and so exactly imitated that one cannot distinguish the true from the false. That it is almost impossible to do here, there not being clever enough people of that type. But even if there were some counterfeits they could not remain long without being recognized. To prevent this abuse one has only to change the dies, and shape of the cards every year after the departure of the vessels for France.

It is true that the colony of Canada will suffer somewhat by these cards, it being quite certain that it will buy French merchandise cheaper if it pays for them in coined money and not in cards, for which the merchants receive only bills of exchange which for the most part are not met at maturity. But it is proper that the colony of Canada suffer for the sake of the kingdom from which it receives all its benefits, and it is only fair that this kingdom should run no risk of losing its money by the possible loss of its vessels bound for it . . . .

RAUDOT [INTENDANT]

*95. "STATUTE CONCERNING FOREIGN COMMERCE IN THE COLONIES, PARIS, JULY 23, 1705" (*Édits et Ordonnances Royaux*, Vol. 1, pp. 425-27).

The King, being informed that foreign commerce continues in some of his colonies despite repeated injunctions . . . and desirous of ending this disorder and conserving . . . to his subjects all the commerce of the colonies . . . , ordains

1 — . . . All Frenchmen and foreigners engaging in prohibited commerce within his American colonies are to be seized by force of arms . . . .

2 — His Majesty permits . . . his subjects . . . to be issued letters of Marque . . . to pursue the ships . . ., reduce them by force of arms, . . . to seize and bring them to the closest lands . . . .

5 — The captures made by His Majesty's subjects will be adjudged to belong to the capturer less $\frac{1}{10}$ reserved to the admiralty, and of the profits realized $\frac{1}{5}$ will be set aside . . . of which $\frac{1}{2}$ will be employed for

the maintenance . . . of hospitals . . . and the remaining half will be allotted ⅔ to the Governor . . . and the other third to the Intendant . . . .

LOUIS

*96. "REPORT OF JACQUES RAUDOT, INTENDANT, . . . ON THE GROWTH OF SEIGNIORIAL ABUSES IN CANADA, NOVEMBER 10, 1707" (Munro, *Seigniorial Documents*, pp. 70-80).

*   *   *

As there are few contracts made in legal form, the notaries, bailiffs, and even judges being almost all ignorant, there is no holding against which some action may not be taken regarding boundaries . . . no guardian who may not be subjected to litigation. . . . It is not that there is bad faith but rather the ignorance and the too few rules that have been followed cause these disorders.

For these reasons . . . I believe that the best interests of the tenants of this country would be served if his Majesty would issue a declaration assuring property rights . . . to those who have inhabited the lands for five years or who have laboured upon them . . . And . . . an act which would validate all existing . . . contracts . . . except . . . odious ones . . . in which usury, . . . fraud, . . . or abuse of authority exists . . . .

. . . Several tenants have held their grants on a verbal agreement from their seigniors, and others have written agreements that do not specify the dues. From this there has arisen much abuse in that tenants who had worked the lands without valid title have been subjected to onerous rents and dues . . . the tenant having the choice of paying these exactions or losing the benefits of his labour . . . .

RAUDOT

*97. "THE EDICTS OF MARLY, JULY 6, 1711" (Munro, *Seigniorial Documents*, pp. 91-94).

The King . . . , informed that among the lands granted in seigniory to his subjects in New France, there are some that are not entirely occupied and others . . . that have not been developed at all . . . [and] His Majesty is also informed that some seigniors . . . refuse to grant lands . . . so that they may sell them . . . which is contrary to His Majesty's intentions . . . ,

. . . orders that within one year of the date of publication of this edict . . . the inhabitants of New France to whom lands in seigniory have been granted . . . that are uncleared . . . must cultivate them . . . failing which . . . His Majesty wishes these lands reunited to his domain . . . .

*   *   *

The King . . . , informed that there are lands which have been conceded to the tenants of New France which are not inhabited nor cleared
. . . , orders that within one year . . . the tenants of New France who do
not occupy the lands granted to them . . . and cultivate them . . . will be
dispossessed . . , the lands to be reunited to the domain of the seignior
. . . .

PHELYPEAUX

D

THE SOVEREIGN COUNCIL

The supreme legislative and judicial body in New France was the
Sovereign Council, which is also sometimes called the Superior Council. Disputes over the prefixes Sovereign or Superior arose over interpretations of its authority. At times, it claimed powers above those of
the governor and the intendant, and presumptuously vied for authority
with the King. The role of the Council in Canadian society is defined,
albeit unclearly, in Documents 98 and 99.

The value of the deliberations and decisions of the Council lies in
the insights they provide into the structure of New France. The compo-
sition of the Council—that is, governor, intendant, senior ecclesiastic,
attorney-general, and councillors—indicates the men and groups possessing power. Their decisions reflected the interests and values of the
élites of Canadian society.

Another evident feature of the French Régime illustrated by these
selections was the paternalism of the period. A modern synonym for
this paternalism would be state intervention. Their concern with, and
control of, the minutiae of daily life is too often emphasized at the
expense of their influence over the chief administrators and the more
significant powers at their disposal.

The governors and intendants of New France were strangers and
transients. In office they would be dependent on the more experienced
permanent residents. Many of these were to be found in the Council.
For example, the implementation of the Edicts of Marly were the concern of the intendant *and the Council*. The members of the Council

were also prominent seigniors. The results were that the Edict concerning the reunion of the lands of the seigniors was not applied until 1740. In the same period over 400 *censitaires,* small tenant farmers, were dispossessed.

The extent of their powers, and the control they exercised over the society, is illustrated in Documents 100 to 104. They range from price control to double morality standards: one for men and another for women.

*98. "COLBERT TO FRONTENAC, ST. GERMAIN, APRIL 20, 1680" (*R.A.P.Q.*, 1926-1927, pp. 112-13).

... His Majesty ... has ordered me to forcibly express his intentions by telling you first that he hopes that you will modify your conduct ..., for His Majesty sees clearly that you lack that spirit ... of compromise so necessary to avoid all the divisions that arise in the country, and which are the principal cause of the loss and ruin of new colonies.

Last year His Majesty informed you of his intentions on the many ill-founded pretensions you held regarding your rights in religious ceremonies. This year a new pretension has arisen with regards to the Sovereign Council. You claimed that you had been given the position of head and president of the Council. The members of the Council opposed this and you made remonstrances in due form. This caused great division between yourself and the Council, and you employed violence and your authority to exile two councillors and the attorney-general.

The King orders me to tell you that your pretensions on this matter astound him ..., they being absolutely contrary to his will as expressed in his declaration of June 5, 1675 ....

                                                        COLBERT

*99. "LIMITS OF POWERS OF SOVEREIGN COUNCIL, THURSDAY, AUGUST 30, 1685" (*Jugements et Déliberations,* Vol. 2, p. 1021).

The Sovereign Council of New France, in conformity with the judgment of the King's Council of State ... of last March, annuls its judgment of August 16 of last year and all that ensued; orders that merchants will have full freedom to sell their wines and liquors in this city and other areas within the jurisdiction of this Council as they did previously ..., His Majesty ... prohibiting the Sovereign Council to make any regulations . . . in the absence of the governor and the intendant. . . .

DE MEULLES

ROUER DE VILLERAY

100. "PRICES OF GOODS BROUGHT BY THE INDIA COMPANY'S
SHIPS TO BE DELIVERED TO THE INHABITANTS OF QUEBEC,
NOVEMBER 14, 1665" (O'Callaghan, *Colonial History
of the State of New York*, Vol. 9, pp. 36-37).

Quebec

	Livres	Sous	Deniers
Wine per barrel	51		
Brandy per barrel	140		
Vinegar, per ton [tun]	180		
Salt, per barrel	14		
Poitou serge, the ell	4	5	10
Linen de Meslis, the ell	1	9	9
Coarse de Meslis, the ell	1	8	1
Large Biscay axes	1	11	5
Small Axes		19	10

Three Rivers

	Livres	Sous	Deniers
The barrel of Wine	56		
The barrel of Brandy	154		
The barrel of salt	15	8	
Small axes	1	2	

Montreal

	Livres	Sous	Deniers
The barrel of Wine	61		
The barrel of Brandy	168		
The barrel of salt	5.3 [sic]		
Small axes	1.4 [sic]		

*101. "PRICE OF BREAD, FEBRUARY 15, 1677"
(*Jugements et Délibérations*, Vol. 2, pp. 109-10).

. . . The Court . . . orders that until such time as a general survey may
be made, that white bread weighing eleven ounces will be sold for twenty
deniers and a pound of brown bread at two sous, in that a minot of
wheat sells for four livres to four livres, ten sous . . . and that there will
be but three bakers in the city who will be given permission to sell and

retail bread on condition that they always have bread in their shops . . . .

DUCHESNEAU [INTENDANT]

*102. "PENALTY IMPOSED ON AN ADULTRESS, NOVEMBER 17, 1677"
(*Jugements et Déliberations*, Vol. 2, p. 97).

In the case of the King's Prosecutor . . . versus Anne Bauge, wife of Guillaume Corruble . . . accused of leading a scandalous and infamous life . . . And in consideration of the conclusions of the said Prosecutor who . . . was informed by the said Bauge that she was three or four months pregnant . . . The court banishes the said Anne Bauge from this city of Quebec . . . for three years and she is enjoined to keep the ban on penalty of corporal punishment, and with reference to Jacques Defai mentioned in the case as a participant . . . he is condemned to a fine of twenty livres . . . .

DUCHESNEAU

*103. "DEATH PENALTY AND REMISSION, LAST DAY OF DECEMBER,
1680" (*Jugements et Déliberations*, Vol. 2, pp. 455-59).

. . . With reference to the appeal in this court of Jean Rattier . . . appealing the death sentence rendered against him . . . for the murder of Jeanne Couc . . . which sentence was appealed on the last day of October 1679, . . . which condemned . . . Jean Rattier . . . to be conducted to a public place . . . designated by the seignior, and there to be led to a gallows, be hanged and strangled and to remain exposed for twenty-four hours . . . The Council . . . rejects the appeal . . . and declares the said Rattier guilty. . . . At the King's pleasure . . . as there is no executioner, . . . it is ordered that he will be held in prison until an executioner is appointed, or, if he so prefers, he may accept the office of executioner, in which case he will be set free . . . .

"The Last Day of December, 1680"

. . . And in that . . . Jean Rattier has declared that he will accept the office of executioner . . . .

DUCHESNEAU

*104. "ORDONNANCE RE CABARET-HOTELS, MONTREAL, JUNE 23,
1710" (*Ordonnances et Jugements*, Vol. 3, pp. 429-30).

As it is necessary to regulate the number of cabaret-hotels which sell

liquor in the City of Montreal, and as the large number facilitates the
drunkenness of the Indians, surveillance not being possible over a large
number so well as a small number . . .

We prohibit all people from retailing liquor in the City of Montreal,
or in the environment of the City, subject to a fine of 50 livres for the
first offence, and if repeated to a fine of 100 livres and being expelled
from the city.

We order that there will be 19 cabaret-hotels which may retail . . .
liquor . . . to Frenchmen; forbid them to sell liquor . . . to Frenchmen
after nine o'clock at night . . . .

Forbid them as well to give any kind of liquor to . . . Indians. . . .
Order that there will be nine cabarets which may retail beer to the
Indians . . .

Forbid as well . . . the serving of liquor to the Indians after the retreat
has sounded . . . and that the cabarets will be obliged to let the Indians
spend the night if they so request.

The 19 cabaret-hotels must get permission to retail liquor from the
Sieur Deschambault . . . .

RAUDOT

E

WAR

The relating of European Wars to the colonial history of the Americas is traditional, but it can also be misleading. The Wars of the League
of Augsburg which were terminated by the Treaty of Ryswick of 1697,
and the War of the Spanish Succession which was ended by the fateful
Treaty of Utrecht of 1713, have their counterparts in the Americas. The
former was called King William's War and the latter Queen Anne's
War. War in New France, however, was a constant from 1680 to 1713.
European conflicts were reflected in America, but American conflicts
also had American causes.

In 1680 the Iroquois attacked the Illinois. This marked the beginning of the Second Iroquois War. Governor La Barre waged an unsuccessful campaign in 1684, but his successor, the Marquis de Denonville,
in 1687, resumed the hostilities with more success. A high point of the

war on the Southern front was a desperation raid by the Iroquois on the
Montreal suburb of Lachine in 1689. The second phase of this engagement lasted until 1701 when the Treaty of Montreal was signed between
the Iroquois and the French, ending, at long last, the French-Iroquois
conflict begun by Champlain.

Political, economic, and military aspects of the war are evident in
the campaigns of the Canadians against the English on the Hudson's
Bay. The exploits of the Le Moyne's were partly military and partly
economic. They began with the successful raids of 1684, and ended, in
spite of Canadian victories, with the retrocession of the Bay to the
English in 1713.

On the Eastern front the French and Canadians were less successful.
Port Royal was captured by William Phips in 1690, handed back to the
French in 1697, and captured again in 1710. From these Eastern bases
the British-Americans launched two campaigns against Quebec: Phips
in 1690 and the Walker Expedition in 1711. Both failed.

The wars of New France in this period are usually associated with
the second governorship of Louis de Buade, Comte de Frontenac. It is
well, however, to remember that they began before the end of his first
tenure, and were terminated after his death. Documents 105 and 106
indicate the role he was to play and the policies to be followed. The
strategy was that of Canadians and the French Court and not that of
Frontenac. The proposed conquest of the Colony of New York was never
undertaken. However, the French were more successful against the
English on the Hudson's Bay. The Pastoral letter of the Bishop, Document 107, was written when Quebec was threatened by the English
and gives an insight into the relations of Church and State in times of
war.

The claims of the English and the French, and, in general, the question of sovereignty over the Iroquois, are the subject-matter of the
following three selections. The significance of the Iroquois lands lay in
their location on the flanks of either the English or French, and the
expansion of either colony to the South-west. York's report, although
slightly erroneous, and those of Bellomont, the governor of New York,
emphasize accurately the predicament of the European foes.

Document 110 foreshadows the Treaty of Utrecht. The significance
to New France of the proposed cession of the Hudson's Bay, Acadia, the
Iroquois, and the fishing stations of Newfoundland is noted. A more
personal note is evident in the Minister's letter to Madame Vaudreuil,
the governor's wife.

The last selection is from the pen of the Baron de La Hontan, a
French soldier who had served in New France and Newfoundland and

then sold his services to the English. It is remarkably astute, for his assessment of the French holdings in America well indicate the ultimate consequences of their loss to France.

*105. "MEMOIR TO SERVE AS INSTRUCTIONS TO . . . FRONTENAC ON THE ENTERPRISE AGAINST NEW YORK, JUNE 7, 1689" (*R.A.P.Q.*, 1927-1928, pp. 12-16).

The King has had examined the proposal made to him by the Sieur Chevalier de Callières, governor of Montreal, to attack New York with troops that His Majesty maintains in Canada and a number of the inhabitants of the country. He has . . . consented for he knows that the inhabitants of those lands have, for the past few years, incited the Iroquois nations . . . to make war on the French. That, to this effect, they have supplied them with arms and ammuntions and, in spite of the orders of the King of England and treaty provisions, have used every means to usurp the commerce of the French in the lands which the latter have always possessed.

*   *   *

His Majesty wishes that he will execute what herein follows:

*   *   *

His Majesty does not wish that he leave in that colony any inhabitants who may be suspect . . . .

*   *   *

He will examine the means to sell the seized effects so that the returns may be used by His Majesty for rewards to those inhabitants, officers . . . soldiers, and sailors who will have distinguished themselves . . . .

*   *   *

If, amongst the inhabitants of New York, English or Dutch, there be Catholics in whose fidelity he may trust, he may leave these in the possession of their habitations after having them swear loyalty to His Majesty as long as they are not too many in number . . . .

He may retain, if he judges it necessary, artisans and others necessary to the cultivation of the lands, or to work on the fortifications, as prisoners. . . .

The officers and principal inhabitants should be kept in prison until they are ransomed.

As for others . . . men, women, and children, His Majesty believes it necessary that they be expelled from the colony and sent to New England, Pennsylvania, and other areas that he may choose, . . . either singly or in groups, whichever way is surest to disperse them and prevent them from re-establishing themselves and occasioning enemy endeavours against the colony.

*106. "MEMOIR OF THE KING TO . . . FRONTENAC ON . . . THE
ATTACK ON PORT NELSON IN THE NORTHERN BAY, THE
CAMP BEFORE MONS, APRIL 7, 1691"
(*R.A.P.Q.*, 1927-1928, pp. 55-56).

*   *   *

On what . . . Frontenac and . . . Champigny have made known of the importance of Fort Nelson usurped . . . by the English . . . and the approbation they have given to the proposals of the Company of the North to attack this fort under the leadership of . . . d'Iberville, a Canadian gentleman, His Majesty has resolved to use the ship *le Hazardeux* in this enterprise commanded by the Sieur du Tast whom his Majesty sends to Quebec. His Majesty has thought it best to leave to . . . Frontenac . . . the giving of the necessary orders for the attack on the Fort by . . . du Tast and d'Iberville . . . .

*107. "PASTORAL LETTER TO PREPARE THE PEOPLE OF THIS DIO-
CESE TO WELL DEFEND THEMSELVES AGAINST THE ENGLISH,
QUEBEC, 1689-1690" (*Mandements des Évêques*, Vol. 1,
pp. 265-67).

You are sufficiently informed of the strange calamities with which we are all menaced by the approach of the English, enemies not only of the French, but of our faith and holy religion. Is it possible that, loving you tenderly as I do and holding you all to my bosom, I should not tremble at the thought of the ravages that might be wreaked among us by the heresy should Divine justice but once permit that fire to be kindled in the hearts of your children? Raise your eyes higher, my Dearly Beloved Children, and see God holding the bolt he is prepared to strike us with; he makes it thunder to draw you from the sloth of sin into which you have fallen, and which has angered him. All he wishes is that you return to him and that by penance you avoid the condemnation he has pronounced against you. Do not be deaf to so terrible a voice. The merchants should not delude themselves in their commerce, nor sleep with their heads under pillows to assuage their consciences. The usurer should not delude himself hastening, on many pretexts, to gain interest on his money, for God declares that he views this commerce as an abomination. The vindictive should renounce their vengeance and be disposed not only to see their enemy but to love him cordially and to do him well. The immodest should stop their disorders, but above all, the sacrilegious sinners must cease desecrating their God by the reiterated profanities of all that is most sanctified and holy in our religion. You understand well enough what I mean, my Dearly Beloved Children. These reproaches are all too well founded . . . .

* * *

I invite you to well protect our shores and exert yourselves to protect the entrance of our city. . . . Before finishing, permit me to recommend to you obedience to your established authorities as to God himself. . . . These are the wishes of a father whose affection grows for you day by day, and who holds you to his bosom so that you may enter that of Our Lord Jesus Christ to whom all glory, honour, and praise for ever and ever, and whosoever does not love him, anathema to him.

JEAN

108. "INFORMATION FURNISHED BY SAMUEL YORK RESPECTING THE WESTERN INDIANS, ALBANY, SEPTEMBER 2, 1700" (O'Callaghan, *Documentary History of the State of New York*, Vol. 4, pp. 748-51).

* * *

. . . I was taken prisoner in Casco Bay in New England by a party of French and Indians under the command of Monsieur de Portneuf in the month of May 1690 and carried to Canada where, and in the hunting Indians countries I have lived ever since till the 29th. day of this last July that I made my escape to come hither, and during the last two years & half I was employed in cutting masts for the use of the French King's navy. There have been ninety great masts cut and sent from thence to France every year by order of the King, the Bay of St. Paul, which is fifteen leagues below Quebec, being the place principally where the sd. masts were cut and shipped. I have often heard that Mons'g de Callière, the Governor of Canada, has pretended a right to the Five Nations of the Indians otherwise called Iroquois, and I was once present in Council when there was an embassy or message to the sd. Governor by some of those Indians, about a fortnight before my coming from Montreal, and then heard him tell the said messengers that the King, his master, had an undoubted right to the Senecca, Onondaga and Oneida Nations, and that he would have them, let it cost what it would. . . . Several of the **French Coureurs de Bois, or hunters,** are there at this time and refuse to obey orders to come to Canada, and are in some sort of rebellion; they **are very desirous to come and trade here with the English,** only fear of **the Five Nations will not suffer them to pass through their country. . . .**

I have often heard the Ottawas express a longing desire to trade with the English in these plantations. The French of Canada are not able to furnish those people with goods . . . and [they] are therefore impatient of being confined to the narrow trade with them. The French have a few Jesuits among those nations, but they seem not to be fond of them. The present Governor of Canada is very severe and not at all beloved by the French or Indians. The people of Canada are all divided into factions and a general discontent among 'em; and there has been a very great scarcity of all provisions, especially of bread, all last winter and this summer . . . .

SAMUEL YORK

his ⋂ mark

109. "EARL OF BELLOMONT TO THE LORDS OF TRADE, NEW YORK, OCTBER 24, 1700" (O'Callaghan, *Documentary History of the State of New York*, Vol. 4, pp. 768-69).

. . . Our Indians, when I was now last at Albany, said they had lost 120 men since the peace; and I remember at my coming hither, which was just at the end of the war, the number of fighting men in the Five Nations was reckoned but 1400 at most. I appeal to your Lordship whether the Five Nations can at this rate last many years and be a barrier between these Plantations and the French. 'Tis the French, without all doubt, that instigate those remote nations to vex and destroy ours as they do. Our nations firmly believe it, and so do I, because the Governor of Canada told some of our Indians so, as your Lordship have been acquainted. We shall lose the Five Nations and all our American Plantations by our frugality; there's no care taken to fortify Albany and Schenectady, either for our own security or for the encouragement of the Indians; so that truly I fear their dread of the French will make 'em revolt to 'em. If 7 or £8,000 sterling is to be put in balance with our keeping these Plantations, then we had as good to make the French a compliment of 'em, before they take 'em from us against our will, as most certainly they will do, if they kill part of our Indians and inveigle away the rest . . . .

BELLOMONT

*   *   *

110. "MEMORIAL OF THE RIGHTS OF THE BRITISH CROWN OVER THE NEW YORK INDIANS, JUNE 2, 1709" (O'Callaghan, *Colonial History of the State of New York*, Vol. 5, pp. 75-77).

*   *   *

From the first settlement of the Colony of New York (which we take to have been about the year 1610) the Five Nations of Indians . . . have by many acknowledgements, submissions, leagues or agreements, been united to, or depended upon that Colony.

*   *   *

The French having endeavoured fruitlessly to draw them into their interests by sending several Missionary Priests among them (from whence they pretend to derive their Ancientest Title to that country, and extend it even as far as the Bay of Mexico) did about forty years ago make an attempt to reduce them by force . . . but the French were constrained by the extremity of the cold weather and want of provisions, to return without effecting anything . . . .

Some time after this, a trading French man, under pretence of mending Indian arms, obtained leave of those Five Nations, to set up a small house and a shop for that purpose, at a place called Cataraqui, near the east entrance of a large lake of the same name; and about the year 1680 . . . the French built a stone fort at the same place.

*   *   *

In the year 1684, upon notice that Monsr. De La Barre, the Governor of Canada, was to come down to Cataraqui, with intent to fall upon the Indians; Colonel Dongan, then Governor of New York, wrote to him that those Indians are the King of England's subjects . . . .

*111. "THE MINISTER TO VAUDREUIL AND BÉGON, MARLY, JUNE 26, 1712" (*R.A.P.Q.*, 1947-1948, pp. 148-50).

I write you this letter, Gentlemen, which must be kept confidential and which must be divulged to no one. Several people of Canada have this year, and specially . . . Vaudreuil and Raudot, represented to me that it will be impossible in the future to maintain the troops from the funds available unless the treasurer . . . redeems the letters of exchange . . . and that the great quantities of card money issued in the country have lowered the value of the former so that there has been a four-fold increase in the price of merchandise . . . I am convinced of the truth of the matter, but the sad state of the Kingdom these past years has prevented His Majesty from meeting . . . the expenses arising from the defence of his Kingdom against the enemies of the state. It is true that this situation may change and that a peace treaty may soon be arrived at, but this will not place His Majesty in a position to redeem all that is owed . . . in Canada . . . .

*   *   *

As peace negotiations have been undertaken, and His Majesty may cede Plaisance to the English, and that the latter may not want to return Acadia, I wrote . . . Vaudreuil last spring . . . urging that it be recaptured. I hope that this enterprise succeeded, but if not, it should no longer be attempted. If Plaisance and Acadia remain in English hands it appears necessary to me to establish other fishing stations. I believe one could be established on Cape Breton Island and the other on the coast of Labrador. I have already been informed on the former. I do not know, however, at what port we could make the establishment . . . .

* * *

The English, in the peace negotiations, will make claims upon us on the capture of the Hudson's Bay. . . . It will be necessary to oppose these.

In 1688, before the war was declared, the English captured a French vessel in the port of Chibouctou, loaded with merchandise . . . .

I am told that the Sieur de la Tour, lieutenant . . . presently in Canada, was plundered in the port of Boston by an English vessel although he had a permit from the governor. It is necessary that you send me a declaration made before a notary to this effect stating the total value of what was seized from him . . . .

*112. "MINISTER TO MADAME DE VAUDREUIL, VERSAILLES, DECEMBER 18, 1712" (*R.A.P.Q.*, 1947-1948, p. 192).

I received, Madame, your letter of the ninth . . . requesting the appointment, as a lieutenant in the navy, of your son in spite of the fact that it was not the King's intention to make any . . . promotions this year in the colonies.

I must admit that your request appeared premature and that I could not, in spite of my desire to please you, propose it to His Majesty.

Moderation in all things is necessary, for His Majesty would not be pleased by too frequent demands. You will always find me disposed to contribute to the advancement of your children when I may do so with justice. I am, respectfully, Madame, your very humble and obedient servant . . . .

113. "INSTRUCTIVE SUMMARY OF THE AFFAIRS OF CANADA, 1696(?)" (Lanctot, *Oakes Collection*, pp. 21, 23-25, 35, 39, 57-59).

* * *

Canada returns nothing directly to the King of France, since the sums accruing from the beaver lease and the import of goods and the export of all kinds of furs are used to maintain forty companies of marines, a governor general, four local ones, an intendant, a sovereign council, and a hundred other officers of justice, a bishop and all his clergy, two or three seminaries, as many hospitals, seven or eight convents of either sex, thirty missions among the Indians, besides the cost of a large amount of munitions; yet that country is of indirect advantage to him, inasmuch as France has only to send ships to Muscovy to trade there with the skins, while at the same time the Indians consume a quantity of goods made in the kingdom, in exchange for the beavers, martens, foxes, otter, and moose which would have to be procured from foreign countries.

THE TRADE OF CANADA

Canada subsists partly on the trade in all kinds of furs which the merchants of that country are free to send to France, to their correspondents, in exchange for the goods they receive thence; the beaver trade is by contract in the hands of the Farmers-General, who alone can ship the skins to their profit, thus all who are in possession of them must bring them to the office of the said parners, where the store-keepers weigh them and reckon how much the agent or director shall give to each in bills of exchange on La Rochelle in payment of the said beaver. Although any amount of furs are imported from Canada, most of the ships would return empty but that some are laden with wheat and peas for France and others with boards and coal for the American Islands, or with cod from Newfoundland for shipment to Spain and Portugal. The merchants of Canada sell their goods at an excessive price to the inhabitants of the coasts or villages, as well as to the Indians of the colony, and so become rich and opulent in a few years, because the money sent thither by the King of France for the maintenance of his troops, by passing through the hands of the peasants who board them during the winter, falls into the coffers of the said traders who keep it from circulating further . . . .

THE INJURY WHICH THE IROQUOIS WAR
CAUSED TO CANADA

The Iroquois are braver, wiser, and more skilful in the trade of war than all the other Indian nations. They consist of five cantons, to wit: Onodagas, Senecas, Cayugas, Oneidas, and Mohawks, which are united somewhat like the Dutch or the Swiss, and though rather distant one from another they are nevertheless so completely bound by common interests that they form but one body . . . .

The English have every reason for assisting them, as well as for the benefit of trade, as that they keep New England safe from attack by the French and even by their Indian friends and allies. . . . The war they make in Canada has destroyed one half of the colony, stripped it of men and cattle, impoverished the richest inhabitants. It prevents the obtaining of beaver from the great trade carried on with them in time of peace, passage by the lakes on the way to the Ottawas, Illinois and Miamis; the making of forts, the building of ships, the ascent of the Grand River save with large escorts, which are often slaughtered in the portages and the rapids of this difficult route, and the descent of our Indians to Montreal to trade their peltries.

*   *   *

OUTLINE OF A PROJECT TO CAPTURE QUEBEC AND PLACENTIA

. . . To make oneself master of New France one must first seize Quebec, then all the other places which are dependent upon it, being only fortified by simple palisades, will be obliged to lay down arms as they are enclosed in the upper part of the River St. Lawrence, . . . in a word, in taking Quebec you take the whole country at the same time.

*   *   *

THE IMPORTANCE OF PLACENTIA TO THE FRENCH

It is the only port in the whole of America whence the French can obtain dried cod in time of war, since the other places, namely St. Pierre [and] Ile Percée are open harbours. . . . Besides that, Placentia is the route of the ships that come from France to Canada . . . .

THE IMPORTANCE OF PLACENTIA TO THE ENGLISH

In the first place, the French would have no more dried cod, unless they would buy it from the English through neutral nations. Secondly, the latter would alone supply all of Spain, Portugal, and Italy, which would bring England considerable profits. Thirdly, it would be a refuge for English privateers, which would bar to the French the entrance to the Gulf of St. Lawrence which is close enough to Placentia, while those from Boston might cruise in the mouth of the said river, so that no vessel could go or come to Canada any more than to Acadia which did not run the risk of being captured. Finally, this place belonging to the English would add to their trade, would cause a great consumption [of goods], would furnish a place for the crews and for the merchants to enrich themselves, while those in France, to whom there remains only that trade and the beaver and the sugar trade, would be ruined and would end by losing them entirely.

PART IV

1713-1760

The year 1713 was a portentous one for New France. The Treaty of Utrecht truncated the colony and threatened to isolate it on the continent. France, and New France, as a result of the wars, faced severe economic recessions which were aggravated by a drastic devaluation of their currencies. Yet the period from 1713 to 1749, a period of peace after a fashion, was notable for the tremendous progress of the colony.

New France, if it was to survive, could not passively accept the cessions of the Treaty of Utrecht. The losses in the East endangered communications with France and denied to the colony a source of wealth which was derived from supplying food and equipment to the fishing fleets. The loss of Acadia, while not in itself disastrous from an economic point of view, did place the English, and the hated New Englanders, in an advantageous military position. It also involved abandoning the Abenaki, with whom the Canadians had an alliance. These Indians had rendered good service to the Canadian cause in past wars by a series of guerrilla raids on the Eastern front. The prestige of the French and the Canadians was another factor. The abandonment of Indian allies would be interpreted as a sign of weakness by other tribes and the cumulative effects would be dangerous to the Canadian-Indian alliance system.

The retrocession of the Hudson's Bay was a severe blow to Canadian ambitions in the North. The Company of the North and the larger Company of Canada had served not only economic but political and military ends with their endeavours in this area. The English, after

1713, could again drain furs and allies from New France through this northern post.

In the South, the Treaty of Utrecht ceded the sovereignty over the Iroquois to the English. The results of this were to threaten Canadian communications with the Mississippi area, allow the British Americans to expand into the Ohio Valley and to place the New York fur traders in a position to sap the trade of the South-west.

Thus, New France in 1713 faced a three-pronged pincer movement. The great difference between 1713 and 1763 was that the Treaty of Utrecht, unlike the Treaty of Paris which ended the Seven Years War, left New France linked to its metropolis. For fifty years this would be the colony's salvation.

Rapid geographic and economic expansion were a matter of survival for the colony. This was facilitated by the administrators of the colony, all of whom served long terms of office. Michel Bégon, the intendant, was in Canada from 1710 to 1726, and Gilles Hocquart, a successor, served from 1729 to 1748. The first Marquis de Vaudreuil was governor from 1705 to 1725. His successor, Charles, the Marquis de Beauharnois, ruled from 1726 until 1747. The Comte de Maurepas, the French Minister of Marine, held that office from 1723 to 1749. The long tenures of these men permitted the initiation and development of stable and continuing policies.

The first theme of this era of Canadian history concerns the immediate reactions of the Canadians, and the French Court, to the Treaty of Utrecht. Theme B, on the economy of New France, first presents the economic crisis and then the rapid development of the commercial system. It is in this period that some of Talon's plans for a diversified Canadian economy were finally realized.

The short third theme is a characterization of the Canadians by three eye-witnesses. The fourth section, on the Canadian Church, presents evidence of some old and continuing quarrels, but at the same time details the social role of the clergy of New France. The last theme deals with the Conquest of New France.

A

THE CONSEQUENCES OF
UTRECHT AND EXPANSION

Document 111 details the cessions of the French to the English. However, it appears that the French had some afterthoughts, for the retention of Cape Breton Island, soon to be renamed Ile Royale, and the restriction of Acadia to its ancient limits, became the bases for new French establishments. A settlement was made at Louisbourg in 1713 and within one year it was made an official colony. Within a few years the construction of the Fortress of Louisbourg was begun.

In the following documents the first Marquis de Vaudreuil, an experienced soldier, Canadian by choice, and then governor of New France, underlines the consequences of the nefarious treaty. The policies he advocated pass well beyond the merely political or military. The Vaudreuil family belonged to the secular aristocracy and were involved not only in the army and administration of the colony, but in the commerce of New France as well. His defence of the fur trade in Document 115 indicates the links between commerce and survival.

The returns of the trade of forts Frontenac and Niagara present statistically the significance of military and commercial outposts. The following documents, an exchange between the interim governor of New France and the governor of New York, graphically present the rivalry of the Canadians and the English in the South-west.

The Canadian response to the Treaty of Utrecht was continental, and this is nowhere better seen than in the continued French attempts to encompass the South-west or Mississippi region. Following in the footsteps of Marquette, Jolliet, and LaSalle, the LeMoyne family of Longueuil struck Canadian roots in the soil of the lower Mississippi. The settlements and forts served multiple purposes: trade, communication, and strategy. French and Canadian policy in this period was directed to the restriction of the British-Americans to the Atlantic shoreline, if possible. And French and Canadian control of the interior was a means of achieving this end. At first the Mississippi area was officially attached to New France. In 1717 the Illinois country and the whole of the Mississippi area was erected as a separate colony. The Canadians, however, were to play a most significant role in its history, for no fewer than three Canadians—Iberville, de Bienville Le Moyne, and Pierre de Rigaud de Vaudreuil—were to be governors of the colony. Documents 120 to 122 illustrate this continental expansion.

The explorations of La Vérendrye in documents 123 to 127 represent the Canadian response to the challenge of the Hudson's Bay and New France's search for new sources of furs. The hesitancy of the French State to underwrite Canadian expansion is very evident. At the same time the needs of New France are nowhere better expressed than in the correspondence of the governors. The failure of France to appreciate the Canadian vision of continental strategy was a significant factor in the eventual loss of the colony.

*114. "THE MINISTER TO VAUDREUIL, VERSAILLES, APRIL 30, 1713"
(*R.A.P.Q.*, 1947-1948, pp. 201-2).

*   *   *

By the same treaty His Majesty ceded to the Kingdom and the Queen of Great Britain the Bay and Straits of Hudson with all the lands, seas, rivers, and grounds dependent upon them . . . and it was agreed . . . that commissioners will be named . . . to determine, within one year, the respective limits of the Hudson's Bay and the lands belonging to France . . . .

His Majesty . . . ceded Acadia to England, in conformity with its ancient limits, as well as the Island of Newfoundland and adjacent islands. . . . His Majesty has reserved but the Island of Cape Breton and all other islands located in the mouth and Gulf of the Saint Lawrence River.

*115. "MEMOIR OF VAUDREUIL TO THE DUC D'ORLEANS, REGENT
OF THE KINGDOM, FEBRUARY, 1716"
(*R.A.P.Q.*, 1947-1948, pp. 291-95).

The Marquis de Vaudreuil, Governor-General of Canada, persuaded that your Royal Highness is convinced of the necessity of conserving this colony, will not present here all the reasons for so doing; he will only attempt to inform him . . . of the means of so doing.

One of the surest means is to prevent the imminent danger to which the colony would be exposed should a new war take place with the English.

This is easily understood when one considers that there are presently in Canada but 4,484 inhabitants between the ages of 14 and 60 capable of bearing arms.

*   *   *

One cannot doubt for an instant that at the first rupture between France and England, the English will make every effort to possess all of Canada and consequently all of North America from which would follow the loss of Mexico from which they would chase the Spanish without any resistance within a few years.

They have also revealed their intentions by the armaments they made in 1711, and even since the peace, and by article 22 of the instructions given by the City of London to their representatives . . . requesting that they demand of the minister of the preceding government, why they left Canada to France, and Cape Breton Island, presently called l'Isle Royale.

If this Island . . . be ceded to the English, and the rest of Canada, there would remain no resources for the cod fisheries, which would result in a considerable loss to the Kingdom.

One cannot express to what point the power of England would augment if she acquired North America and how this power would be felt in Europe.

This should suffice to show the necessity there is to profit from the peace to fortify Canada by sending people to complete the infantry companies as well as to augment the number of inhabitants.

*   *   *

One of the primary concerns of the Marquis de Vaudreuil . . . has been keeping the peace with the Indians and preventing them, as much as possible, from trading with the English.

*   *   *

The Marquis de Vaudreuil thus hopes that your Royal Highness will send to Canada this year . . . thirty thousand livres of presents for the Indians . . . .

*116. "VAUDREUIL AND BÉGON TO THE MINISTER, QUEBEC, SEP-
    TEMBER 20, 1714" (*R.A.P.Q.*, 1947-1948, pp. 272-88).

*   *   *

We have the honour, Monseigneur, to inform you, as we did last year, of the necessity . . . to permit at least for a few years, freedom to trade in the hinterland, and for several reasons.

The first is that commerce in general should not be restrained and that a merchant may better achieve his aims in freedom than in constraint.

The second is that if everyone is free to trade those who do not make a profit on their first voyage will abandon the matter and it follows that they will not then return to the hinterland. Thus only the number necessary to bring the trade goods will go . . . .

The third is that presently there are in the hinterland at least two hundred coureurs de bois who, not having any other profession, . . . could never be compelled to remain in the settled areas no matter what punishments or chastisements are threatened.

The fourth is that the men of this profession should be considered as useful to the colony as much for their abilities in times of war . . . as for the merchandise they bring to the Indians who will then not trade with the English . . . , which must be considered a great advantage as the Indian's loyalty is bought by fulfilling their needs and they will always favour those with whom they trade.

The fifth is that, putting aside the security of the colony, particular attention must be taken to stop the Indians from frequenting the English for fear that they will allure them by all sorts of means. This freedom to trade is an effective means of increasing the fur trade, and consequently, reducing that of the English.

Last . . . , it is necessary to follow this policy to forestall the designs of the English against this colony, of which they speak openly, insinuating to the Indians, that they will be masters of the country. And when we have among these Indians many Frenchmen, we will be informed by them of the enterprises, which is important . . . .

*   *   *

Father Felix . . . has informed Vaudreuil and Bégon that a few inhabitants . . . who went to Isle Royale to examine the possibility of establishing themselves, reported that they were given but two acres of land and that they would not be permitted to sow wheat as all the flour to be consumed on the Island was to be drawn from Canada in order to increase the value of wheat and lands, and that they would be assigned to seigniors to whom they would pay their dues. This had the effect of cooling the ardour they had to establish themselves. They also hope that His Majesty will have the goodness to furnish them for one year . . . with the necessities of life. The sieurs Vaudreuil and Bégon believe, Monseigneur, that if it is His Majesty's wish to establish, in a short time, a considerable colony, the best means of attracting inhabitants would be to give, without charge, for one year, to each family composed of three people a soldier's daily ration and two rations to those composed of six people, and so on proportionally. This help, added to the returns of their labours, would permit them to support their families.

*   *   *

117. "STATEMENT OF THE SKINS DERIVED FROM THE TRADE DONE AT FORT FRONTENAC AND NIAGARA . . . 1722 AND 1723

WHICH HAVE BEEN SOLD AT QUEBEC, QUEBEC, OCTOBER 30, 1723" (Preston and Lamontagne, *Royal Fort Frontenac*, pp. 214-15).

In 1722

	l	s	d
975 Martens at 42s, 6d.	2,071	17	6
228 Pecans at 55s	627		
640 Deer skins-raw and 1 idem of moose at 10 1.	6,410		
4435 pounds of dry Beaver, on which 5% deduction leaves 4216 pounds at 40s	8,432		
168 pounds of fat Beaver, on which 5% deduction leaves 156 pounds 8 ounces at 4 1.	638 ...		

In 1723

	l	s	d
1,004 large and medium bears at 56s	2811	4	
172 Deer skins — raw 6 skins of moose and 1 skin of deer in parchment at 11 1. 10s	2,058	10	
119 bear cubs at 36s	220	3	
2634 cats at 19s	2,503	5	
1036 otters at 56s	2,916		
1290 skins of deer weighing 1,445 pounds at 35s	2,528	15	
48 timber wolves at 50s	120		

Recapitulation

Skins sold in 1722	18,178	17	6
Skins sold in 1723	22,732	11	
Total	40,911	8	6

Expenses

Given in exchange for the said skins — 29,800 livres, 17s, 6d of provisions, munitions, and store goods according to the account attached.

*   *   *

WAGES OF EMPLOYEES FOR THE FUR TRADE

To an agent employed to do the trade at . . . Frontenac	900 livres
To another agent . . . at the head of Lake Ontario	350
To another agent . . . in the Bay of Quinte	350
To another agent . . . at Niagara	400
To six soldiers . . . to help to do the trading . . . 30 livres each	180

*   *   *

Total expenses	35210 livres

Comparison

The sale of the skins amounted to	40,911	livres 8s	6d
and the expenses to	35,210	17	6
Profit	5,700	11	

BÉGON

118. "GOVERNOR BURNET* TO MR. DE LONGEUEIL,† ALBANY, JULY 5, 1726" (O'Callaghan, *Colonial History of the State of New York*, Vol. 5, pp. 802-3).

From the report of persons who have been among the 5 Nations, I have learned that about a hundred Frenchmen were at Niagara commencing the erection of a fort there, with the design of shutting in the Five Nations, and preventing the free passage of the other Indians at that point to trade with us as they have been in the habit of doing; I have considered it my duty to state to you how much I am surprised at an undertaking so opposed to the Treaty of Peace concluded at Utrecht, where it has been stipulated that the 5 Nations shall be left to the English, and that the French shall not molest them in any manner, and that all the Indians in America shall enjoy full liberty of resorting to each of the two Nations to make their trade without any hindrance. I believe, also, that the Five Nations will ever maintain that the lands at Niagara are their property, and that the French have never, in Mr. de Lasalle's time, nor since, undertaken anything in that quarter, in time of peace, without the consent of the Senecas, and inasmuch as the Five Nations have been ceded to us by the French at that last peace, it follows that the latter have no longer any claim to their lands. . . . Should the fortifying [of] Niagara be continued, I shall be under the necessity of representing the matter to my Superiors, in order that the Court of France, being well informed of the fact, may give its opinion thereupon; as I have heard that it has already expressed its disapprobation of the part Mr. de Vaudreuil took in the War of the Abenaquis against New England.

*   *   *

119. "LONGEUEIL TO BURNET, MONTREAL, AUGUST 16, 1726" (O'Callaghan, *Colonial History of the State of New York*, Vol. 5, p. 803).

*   *   *

The Governor General who is coming from France this year will be

---

* Governor of New York.
† Governor of Montreal.

at liberty, should he think proper, to communicate to you the decision
of the Court of France respecting the post at Niagara. . . .

I have no knowledge that the Court disapproved the Marquis de
Vaudreuil's proceedings in relation to the Abenaquis. . . .

*120. "CHARLEVOIX ON LOUISIANA" (Charlevoix, *Histoire de la
Nouvelle France,* Vol. 4, pp. 163-64).

* * *

The French, after having discovered the known course of the River,
do not appear to have paid much attention to the advantages that might
be derived. This indifference continued for nearly thirty years. Finally,
the proximity of the mines of New Mexico, and of those supposedly
discovered in Louisiana itself, having awakened our nation from this . . .
sloth, more men, more money, and more effects were sent from the Kingdom in three years to make an establishment . . . than had been sent
from the times of Francis I for any of our colonies of the New World.

But when it was realized that the country would produce neither gold
nor silver, and that it was difficult to tap the riches which New Spain
held in its bosom, there suddenly arose a general outcry. No attention at
all was paid to the fecundity of the lands, nor to the returns it might
provide with a moderate amount of work, nor to the importance of
establishing a fleet in the Gulf of Mexico. . . .

. . . When d'Iberville left in . . . April 1700 there were no French
habitations in Louisiana other than the few Canadians established
among the Illinois . . . [and] another establishment at Biloxi. . . .

*121. "CHARLEVOIX ON THE UTILITY OF THE ILLINOIS POST"
(Charlevoix, *Histoire de la Nouvelle France,* Vol. 6,
p. 152).

* * *

. . . What appears to be certain is that there are two advantages to be
derived of which one will never be disputed and the other is, for the
moment, necessary to the whole country. The first is related to its location which is close to Canada with whom there will always be communication useful to the two colonies. The second is that it can be the granary
of Louisiana to which it could furnish abundant grains even if Louisiana
were populated as far as the sea.

Not only is the soil capable of bearing wheat, but it has never refused
anything necessary for the feeding of man. The climate is mild . . . it
would be very easy to breed herds . . . and even to domesticate the wild
cattle from which could be derived much profit through the commerce

of wool and leather, and for the feeding of the inhabitants. . . . And finally we are assured of the friendliness of the Illinois. . . . They are almost all Christians, have a gentle nature, and are . . . fond of the French.

*122. "MEMOIR ON THE FRENCH COLONIES ON THE GULF OF MEXICO, PARIS, OCTOBER 4, 1736" (*Collection de Manuscrits*, Vol. 3, pp. 180-81).

* * *

. . . Iberville returned to France, and not having the funds necessary to complete the purchases needed to maintain his projects, addressed himself to . . . Crozat who furnished the funds. But, after all the purchases had been made, . . . and Iberville having died, . . . Crozat continued Iberville's commercial projects . . . and to this effect he obtained a patent from the King. . . .

* * *

. . . Crozat's clerk sold the merchandise at a profit.

But as Crozat did not wish to continue his association with the colony . . . he ceded his privileges to the Company of the Indies. . . .*

And it was after this . . . that the King granted the concession . . . of the country that we today call Louisiana.

This company made immense expenditures, but because of disorders and the lack of a reasonable plan . . . these expenses having produced no fruit . . . it was finally retroceded to the King.

* * *

It is to remedy these conditions that the Sieur de la Boulaye, informed of all the faults made to the present, offers to present a detailed plan . . . of what he considers necessary to render the colony . . . advantageous to the State. . . .

DE LA BOULAYE

123. "BEAUHARNOIS TO MAUREPAS, QUEBEC, OCTOBER 8, 1734" (Burpee, *La Vérendrye*, pp. 110-16).

I have received the letter which you did me the honour to write me on the twentieth of April last, on the subject of the explorations of the Sieur de la Vérendrye. . . .

I have to inform that officer that His Majesty was not disposed to

---

* The Company of the Indies was formed by John Law, a Scottish-born financier and speculator. The Company also monopolized the fur trade of New France.

incur any expenses in the aid of his discovery. He has represented to me
again, and I have knowledge that it is true, that the amount which he
and his associates have spent in order to push forward their establishments is much more than any profit that they have derived from them.
He added that these same associates were not disposed to assume the
further expenses that were necessary for the following out of his project,
but that since the prospect of final success appeared to him in no way
doubtful he had overcome the one really essential obstacle by obtaining
supplies from merchants. . . .

The zeal which the Sieur de la Vérendrye manifests for this enterprise
has seemed to me to proceed alone from a desire to accomplish the discovery of the Western Sea and render his establishment useful to the
colony. It is a matter of established fact that those which he has made in
the countries of the tribes with which the English were carrying on trade
will be of use both in diverting their commerce from English channels
and in increasing the trade in beaver and peltries generally which is
carried on in this colony. . . .

After having had the honour, Monseigneur, of giving you an account
of the measures which the Sieur de la Vérendrye has taken to achieve his
discovery, permit me to beg of you to urge upon His Majesty to bestow
some consideration upon that officer. I venture to assure you that the
zeal which he manifests for this enterprise cannot be suspected of any
other motive than the well-being of the service and of the colony, and
that, up to the present, it has been a very costly thing for him. . . .

124. "MAUREPAS TO BEAUHARNOIS AND HOCQUART, FONTAINE-
     BLEAU, APRIL 17, 1742" (Burpee, *La Vérendrye*, pp.
     289-92).

Since the Sieur de la Vérendrye undertook an overland journey to
discover the Western Sea, the Marquis de Beauharnois has forwarded
to me several journals sent to him by that officer relating to the progress
of his enterprise. If, on the one hand, the details which they contain
give some reason to hope for his success, they show also that it is
necessary to give him some help towards pursuing his object. For this
purpose it has seemed to me that it might be suitable to associate with
him an officer who, by his talents, might be qualified to assist in the
enterprise. An arrangement of this kind is all the more suitable on
account of the importance of training in the colony officers who, by their
conduct and through the knowledge they may acquire of the habits of
the tribes with whom the Sieur de la Vérendrye has established relations,
may later render service in governing them. . . .

125. "MAUREPAS TO BEAUHARNOIS, VERSAILLES, MAY 12, 1745" (Burpee, *La Vérendrye*, pp. 459-60).

*   *   *

The company has been given to the Sieur de la Vérendrye; but the same reasons that prevented His Majesty from assigning him one of those which fell vacant last year have further determined him not to give him seniority over those who were then preferred to him. The reason is that, having for several years been solely occupied with his own affairs, he has done nothing for the service; all those journeyings of his ending in nothing but trade with the savage tribes whose settlements he has frequented. . . .

126. "MAUREPAS TO LA JONQUIÈRE, VERSAILLES, MARCH 6, 1747" (Burpee, *La Vérendrye*, pp. 465-67).

I am replying to the letters written by the Marquis de Beauharnois on the 1st . . . and 18th of October last. . . .

You know that several years ago an attempt was made in Canada to discover the Western Sea by the overland route. The first to be entrusted with the enterprise was the Sieur de la Vérendrye, captain in the troops. He established a number of posts in the far West which enabled him to do a considerable business with the surrounding tribes; but, content with the profits accruing from this trade, that officer was very slacking pursuing the discovery which ought to have been the principal object of his efforts.

*   *   *

It was long the custom in Canada to hand over to the commanders of the posts the whole trade and commerce done there, exacting only a small sum by the way of farming rent; but His Majesty having been informed that the abuses to which this system gave rise, and wishing the merchants of Canada to have the benefit of this trade, gave instructions in 1742 to Messieurs de Beauharnois and Hocquart to farm out all the posts on his behalf, reserving to the officers in charge a certain allowance on the proceeds, to be determined when the lease was made. . . .

127. "LA GALISSIONIÈRE TO MAUREPAS, QUEBEC, OCTOBER 23, 1747" (Burpee, *La Vérendrye*, pp. 468-69).

I hardly thought of replying on the subject of the discovery of the Western Sea, being still insufficiently informed regarding it. I would only say that it appears to me that what has been reported to you with reference to the Sieur de la Vérendrye having bestowed more pains on his own interests than on the explorations is entirely false, and moreover that any officers who may be employed on that task will be under the necessity of giving a part of their attention to commerce as long as the King shall not furnish them with other means of subsistence. . . .

B

THE ECONOMIC EXPANSION OF NEW FRANCE

The period 1713 to 1760 in the history of New France was one of extreme contrasts. At the beginning of the era the colony was near bankruptcy. This was followed by a readjustment which lasted until about 1719. From that date until the end of the War of the Austrian Succession in 1748, the country was blessed with an unparalleled prosperity. The years from 1748 until the Capitulation of Montreal in 1760 were ones of prosperity, runaway inflation, and finally the absolute collapse of the economy.

The writings of Ruette d'Auteuil, an experienced politician and businessman of Canada, indicate the seriousness of the currency problem which arose after the signing of the Treaty of Utrecht. His comments emphasize the bad administration which, without a doubt, was a decided fault. However, the curtailment of the fur market, too-extended borrowing, under-capitalization, and the inflation of the period were also factors. These documents, 128 to 130, also indicate an often overlooked feature of the economy of New France, that is, the indirect benefits accruing to the Kingdom of France from the trade of the colony. There is no doubt that the French treasury expended more money on New France than it received from it. However, the profit-and-loss statement should include a further figure: the profits derived by French businessmen from the trade of Canada.

As the commercial community, and the society of New France, became more complex, the rigid laws prohibiting public bodies from speaking in the name of a group were set aside. Document 131, the creation of a Chamber of Commerce for Canada, indicates this more permissive attitude.

The expansion of the Canadian commercial system was to be noted
in agriculture, the fur trade, the timber trade, shipbuilding, and the
Iron Forges of St. Maurice at Three Rivers.
As yet, a price index for the French Régime in Canada has not been
established. Document 132, a lottery inventory, is an attempt to indicate
the current valuations of goods in the period under consideration. The
following document concerns the wage rate, and what might be called
a production speed-up.
The censuses of Canada of 1720 and 1734, Document 134, evidence
numerically the progress of the period. There was an evident population growth, but this is overshadowed by the proportionally greater
increase of productive lands, and the even more rapid and diversified
increase of products of the soil. The profits to be derived from commercial agriculture explain, in part, the resistance of the administrators
of New France to the implementation of the Decrees of Marly indicated
in Documents 135 and 136. Many seigniors, aware of the future value
of land, held their grants for speculative purposes.
Another feature of the growth of commercial agriculture was the
use of New France as the principal supplier of foodstuffs for the Fortress
of Louisbourg. The Royal will is evidenced in Document 137, and the
following selection lists the products supplied, and the prices paid by
the French State to the Canadian business men.
The table of "Trade Statistics" and the extracts from the budget of
1743 (Documents 139, 140) indicate not merely growth and development, but, much more important, the role of the metropolis in the
economic life of New France. Particular attention should be paid to
the various provisions of the budget, for, as is obvious, the metropolitan government was a very large purchaser of goods and labour. The
fact that New France had a budgetary deficit should not obscure the
much more important fact that France could, and did, act as an economic pump-primer in the colony.
The remaining documents concern a variety of economic endeavours
which have one factor in common: their initiation and development
was dependent upon the participation of the French State. New France
was fortunate in having as its intendant a man of the calibre of Gilles
Hocquart. He was probably the best intendant in New France during
the French Régime, although he is today little known.
One of the great problems of any colonial society was the establishment of industries. This was specially true of New France, for the small
population did not provide a sufficient market for a profitable industrial system. Metropolitan subsidies were the answer, and Hocquart's
letters indicate the diversity of France's investments in the colony.

The two largest undertakings of the period were the establishment of the shipyards at Quebec and the construction of the St. Maurice Forges. The French State, by loans and direct subsidization, made these endeavours possible. It cannot be too strongly emphasized, again, that although these were not directly profitable to the State, they did provide work, income, and industries to New France.

Documents 141 to 143 concern the economy in a generalized way and illustrate the ideas of the two preceding paragraphs. The St. Maurice Forges are the subject-matter of the remaining selections. The last one, Document 147, is from the pen of the Swedish naturalist and *voyageur*, Peter Kalm, who visited New France in 1749.

128. "GENERAL ACCOUNT OF THE CARD MONEY AND ITS CONSE-
QUENCES, PARIS, DECEMBER 9, 1715" (Shortt, *Currency*,
Vol. 1, pp. 325-35).

* * *

The second cause of the ruin of the trade in Canada comes from the worthlessness of the card money which the Governors and Intendants have put into circulation. . . . What gave occasion to this kind of money was the failure of the King to appropriate funds for the payment of the troops . . . and for war expenses and other unforeseen expenditures. . . . Since, in the beginning, few cards were issued, and . . . were duly paid, one could not fully realize the injuries which might follow. . . . It is also true that if they had been confined within limits of moderation the evil would not have reached the extent it has.

. . . at the time of the departure of M. de Champigny from the Intendancy of the country which was in 1702, there remained at the most only 120,000 livres of this card money. . . .

Since the departure of . . . M. de Champigny, this facility in issuing money led Messrs de Vaudreuil, Governor, Beauharnois and Raudots, father and son, Intendants, to issue it in succession for very large amounts. . . . Although there were in 1712 more than 1,300,000 livres of these cards, . . . Vaudreuil and Bégon issued . . . more than 500,000 livres of new ones, . . .

Things were in this state when . . . Bégon . . . informed certain merchants of Quebec . . . that if they were willing to lose one-half on the cards they had, the other half would be paid them in France . . . to which they submitted, not being able to do better. . . . The pitiable hope of losing only the half of their property when they were contemplating a complete loss did not fail to renew the courage of the merchants. . . .

*129. "MEMOIR TO HIS ROYAL HIGHNESS THE DUC D'ORLEANS,
REGENT OF FRANCE, PARIS, DECEMBER 12, 1715"
(*R.A.P.Q.*, 1922-23, pp. 58-69).

Patriotism is such a common sentiment that all we can hope for is that
those who read this memoir will appreciate the zeal of the Canadian . . .
who wrote it hoping to correct the erroneous, and publicly stated view,
that Canada was worth nothing.

This vast stretch of country is immensely wealthy . . . but restricting
ourselves only to those areas actually inhabited by Frenchmen, and of
the Gulf and Saint Lawrence River linked to the trade with the indigenous inhabitants, we can easily conclude that if the affairs of the country
are in a poor condition it is not due to the nature of the land, but rather
to the poor management of those who have directed the colony. . . .

Commercial endeavours in Canada . . . may be divided into two sections: those involving the indigenous inhabitants and those carried on
independently of them.

Since the first discovery of Canada the trade of European merchandise
for beaver skins has been the most striking commercial endeavour
because of the large profits that may be realized . . . a commerce, that in
some years, has had a value of 5 or 600,000 livres. . . .

As to the commercial endeavours which are carried on independently
of the indigenous inhabitants they are divided as follows.

First there is agriculture, which produces maize, wheat, rye, barley,
peas and other grains, meat, and wood, all of which are loaded on ships
to be sent to the fishing grounds of the Gulf, and presently to Ile
Royale and to the French West Indies.

The second is that which is procured, and can be procured, from the
River and Gulf of the Saint Lawrence . . . cod, salmon, herring, mackerel,
and other fish which can be salted . . . and which can be said, without
exaggeration, to be inexhaustible. . . .

. . . To this must be added the construction of ships . . . and forest
products which can be sent to France for shipbuilding, masts, and planks
. . . , for the forests of Canada can furnish all kinds of wood . . . and the
rivers emptying into the Saint Lawrence facilitate their transportation.
. . .

To this may be added . . . the exploitation of varied mineral reserves,
for there are excellent iron ore deposits, and in a bay called Michigan
and at Lake Huron almost pure copper mines have been found. . . .

No doubt it will be objected: 1—that the country is very cold; 2—that
population growth has been slow; 3—that commerce languishes. . . . The
objections may be answered by saying that the first is not a drawback
and that the inconvenience of the others cannot be blamed on the
country or on the inhabitants, and that their remedy lies at hand. . . .

RUETTE D'AUTEUIL

*130. "ADDITION TO THE MEMOIR WRITTEN IN 1715 WHICH WAS
ENTITLED ON THE PRESENT STATE OF CANADA, PARIS,
JANUARY 25, 1719" (*R.A.P.Q.*, 1922-23, pp. 73-77).

The memoir written in 1715 considered three objections . . . but a
fourth . . . was omitted . . . that Canada costs the King more than it profits
him.

ANSWER

. . . The Secretaries of State have not continued to implement the
decree given by the King . . . on March 5, 1648. . . .

An attentive consideration of this decree . . . indicates that the intent
of the King was that the Governor-General of Canada could be chosen
from amongst the inhabitants of the country as it was expressly stated
that the ex-governor . . . would be a member for three more years of the
Council established at Quebec by the decree. . . .

This was done for sixteen years without increasing the budget . . . and
it would still be implemented if the . . . Secretaries of State did not have
relatives or favourites whom they wish to appoint . . . at large salaries. . . .

The same intent resulted in the appointment of intendants who are
absolute masters of the judicial and police systems and have an inde-
pendent control over the finances although the Council which was established in 1663 could have fulfilled these functions . . . without additional
costs to the King.

The ease with which added costs are attributed to the King has made
the clergy and religious communities so bold . . . as to substantially
add . . . new gratuities and gifts, on any and all pretexts, to the extent
that the larger part of the fixed budget of Canada . . . is in the form of
these gratuities and gifts. . . .

REVENUES OF CANADA, ASSURED

Among those which are assured . . . is the annual payment . . . of
90,000 livres by the owners of the monopoly of the Western Domain
plus 10% of the value of all wines and liquors imported into Canada
as well as five sous for every pound of tobacco.

10% of the value of all caribou skins exported and the monopoly of
the trade with the indigenous inhabitants from the Bay of St. Paul to
Seven Islands . . . and as far north as the Hudson's Bay.

In addition the right to 25% of the value of all beaver skins exported
from Canada . . .

. . . and the duty on all pelts entering France . . . and finally the duties
collected on cod . . . and fish oils . . . produce a large income. . . . These
are the direct revenues produced in Canada . . . ; as to the indirect
revenues:

. . . the utility of Canada to France lies in part in the number of ships engaged either in fishing or commerce which employ a large number of sailors who are then in a position to pay the taxes imposed upon them by the King.

A second source of income is derived from the outfitting . . . of these vessels. . . .

A third is the purchase and shipment of merchandise from many provinces of France for the commerce of Canada which are paid for by the exports of the country and results in an increased circulation of money, a large part of which eventually finds itself in the King's coffers.

CONCLUSIONS

From what has been said it results that nothing necessitates the large expenditures . . . made for Canada. . . .

All that needs be done is to retrench those expenses which are not necessary. . . .

By these means the expenditures in Canada will not be more than 90,000 livres which is what the King receives from his rental of the Western monopoly, . . . and this country would then be profitable to the King. . . .

RUETTE D'AUTEUIL

*131. "DECREE PERMITTING THE MERCHANTS OF THE CITIES OF QUEBEC AND MONTREAL TO ASSEMBLE DAILY . . . TO CONDUCT THEIR BUSINESS AFFAIRS . . . MAY 11, 1717" (*Édits, Ordonnances Royaux*, Vol. 1, pp. 360-70).

. . . The request presented to the King by the merchants of the cities of Quebec and Montreal in New France states that commerce is the principal means by which the colony may prosper and flourish . . . and that it is impossible for it to prosper and flourish so long as the merchants do not have the freedom to assemble to deliberate on their business affairs . . . as they do in France. . . . His Majesty permits . . . the said merchants to assemble daily in a convenient location in each of the said cities of Quebec and Montreal . . . and to appoint in each of the said cities an agent to represent them. . . .

*132. "INVENTORY OF THE EFFECTS OF THE LOTTERY OF . . . THE WIDOW CARCY . . . APRIL 22, 1732" (*R.A.P.Q.*, 1923-24, pp. 150-53).

To Wit	livres	sous	deniers
14 length of maroon cloth	210		
5 length of ¾ drapes, black	86	5	
3 large blankets	90		
6 large hats	27		
2 semi-beaver hats	30		
5 lengths of flannel	19	5	
3 pairs of women's stockings	10	10	
2 pairs of men's shoes	10		
1 pair of slippers	4	10	
6 pairs of women's shoes	30		
1 pair of children's shoes	2	10	
2 dozen pairs of scissors	18		
11 small snuff boxes	5	10	

To Wit	livres	sous	deniers
6 pairs of fine gloves	9		
14 handkerchiefs	17	10	
1 map of the river	3		
1 linen petticoat, embroidered	20		
5 bonnets	20		
3 pairs of beaver gloves	7	10	
1 pair of women's blue silk stockings	7	10	
1 sword with a silver handle	30		
188 pots of molasses	141		
1 pot of pomade	5		

*133. "WAGES AT QUEBEC, QUEBEC, OCTOBER 11, 1739"
(Innis, *Select Documents,* pp. 393-94).

. . . I have had the honour, Monseigneur, of informing you on several
occasions of the high cost of a day's labour. The best are paid 3 livres a
day during the summer by merchants. I have established, but not without
difficulty, that their wages in the King's employ will be 50 sous a day . . . ;
the price of 50 sous will be reduced for winter work beginning the 15 of
this month till April 1, to 40 sous. . . .

There is a means to shorten the object of these day's work and that
is that the workers apply themselves as is the usage, and that they arrive
at their work before the rising of the sun and that they do not leave till
long after its setting.

HOCQUART [INTENDANT]

134. "CENSUSES OF CANADA, 1720 AND 1734"
(*Censuses of Canada,* Vol. 4, pp. 53, 57).

	1720	1734
Population		
Males, married, over 50	1,314	1,718
Males, married, under 50	2,857	4,588
Males, married, age unknown	282	430
Females, married, all ages	4,107	6,593
Males, unmarried, under 15	3,970	8,342
Males, unmarried, over 15	3,513	3,971
Females, unmarried, under 15	5,269	8,122
Females, unmarried, over 15	3,639	3,952
Total	24,951	37,716
Buildings		
Public buildings	67	54
Churches	86	77
Grist mills	90	118
Saw mills	30	52
Arms		
Fire arms	5,263	6,619
Swords	923	774
Lands		
Cultivated, (arpents)	62,145	163,111
Pasture	12,203	17,657

	1720	1734
Domestic Animals		
Horses	5,603	5,056
Horned cattle	23,388	33,179
Sheep	13,823	19,815
Swine	16,250	23,646
Agricultural Products		
Wheat, bushels	282,700	737,892
Barley, bushels	4,585	3,462
Oats, bushels	64,035	163,988
Peas, bushels	57,400	63,549
Corn, bushels	7,205	5,223
Flax, pounds	54,650	92,246
Hemp, pounds	2,100	2,221
Tobacco, pounds	48,038	166,054

*135. "ROYAL INSTRUCTIONS CONCERNING THE ENFORCEMENT OF
THE DECREES OF MARLY, DECEMBER 19, 1721"
(Munro, *Seigniorial Documents*, pp. 166-67).

. . . His Majesty's intention is that . . . those who have concessions . . .

that are not developed . . . will be reunited in conformity with the Decrees of July 6, 1711. . . .

*136. "DISPATCH OF . . . BEAUHARNOIS AND HOCQUART . . . COM-PLAINING OF THE CONDUCT OF VARIOUS SEIGNIORS, AND ASKING FOR A REITERATION OF THE PROVISIONS OF THE DECREES OF MARLY, QUEBEC, OCTOBER 3, 1731" (Munro, *Seigniorial Documents*, pp. 172-74).

. . . If it pleases His Majesty to order again the publication of the Decrees of 1711 . . . and to grant a delay of one or two years to proprietors of seigniories that are not cleared . . . , as to the grants by seigniors to inhabitants, Hocquart has . . . conformed to the Decree of July . . . 1711, and has reunited more than two hundred concessions to seigniorial domains. . . .

*137. "MAUREPAS TO DUPUY, VERSAILLES, MAY 24, 1728" (P.A.C., C 11 A, Vol. 50, f. 556).

* * *

With a view to procuring a greater market for the flour and vegetables of Canada, I had thought that the King might, in the future, supply Louisbourg . . . with supplies . . . from Quebec. . . .

*138. "SUMMARY STATEMENT OF MERCHANDISE FROM CANADA TO LOUISBOURG, 1740" (P.A.C., F 2 B, Vol. 2, 1732-40, 1752-56).

Merchandise	Quantity	Price	Total
Quintals* of milled flour	6,956.9	12 l.	83,483 l. 15s. 2d.
Quintals of whole flour	711.24	10 l.	7,112 l. 8s.
Quintals of whole flour, 2nd. class	1,666.41	9 l. 90d.	15,831 l. 17s. 10d.
Quintals of biscuits	7,500	10 l.	75,000 l.
Quarts† of peas	726	10 l.	7,260 l.

* Approximately 100 pounds.
† Approximately 220 pounds.

Merchandise	Quantity	Price	Total
Quintals of tobacco	63.82	40 l.	2,521 l. 16s.
Quintals of salted pork	8	35 l.	280 l.
Pine planks, 12'	810	15s.	607 l. 10s.
Quintals of nails	40.71	40 l.	1,628 l. 8s.
Quintals of candles	5	60 l.	300 l.
Hogsheads of salted salmon	2	90 l.	180 l.
Hogsheads of eels	4	15 l.	60 l.
. . .			
Little cheeses	9	2 l. 10s.	22 l. 10s.
. . .			
Quintals of iron	95	20	1,900 l.

139. "TRADE STATISTICS OF NEW FRANCE, 1728-1756"
(Lunn, *Economic Development in New France,
1713-1760*, pp. 449, 464-65, 477).*

Year	Flour (bbls.)	Biscuit (quintals)	Peas (bbls.)	Furs (livres)	Exports (livres)	Imports
1728	6,613	11,802	3,760	1,268,866		
1732	6,433	8,858	4,452	1,182,473	1,483,192	1,931,424
1733	2,194	2,847	966	1,150,636	1,389,047	1,631,603
1736	7,054 (quintals)	11,574	4,040	682,108	1,677,696	1,913,542
1739	9,524	10,618	1,827	1,053,178	2,103,864	1,919,572
1740	9,333 (quintals)	7,500	726	1,064,139	2,111,107	2,264,077
1754	366	40	269	382,424		
1756				145,495		

*140. "EXTRACTS FROM THE BUDGET OF NEW FRANCE, 1743"
(P.A.C., *Correspondance Generale*, C 11 A, Vol. 115-1,
f. 60-64).

*　　*　　*

Memoir on the finances of Canada for the year 1743.
The funds provided to be drawn on the King's budget . . . were:

---

* Alice Jean Elizabeth Lunn, *Economic Development in New France, 1713-1760*. Montreal: McGill University, 1942. 495 pp. (Unpublished Ph.D. Thesis). I wish to acknowledge the gracious consent of the parties involved for the use of the above statistics. (CN).

	l	s	d
For the construction and maintenance of boats and canoes . . .	9,300		
For voyages to the interior . . .	4,000		
For freight of foodstuff and other supplies from Quebec to various locations . . .	6,600		
Labour costs and other works . . .	7,300		
For purchase of merchandise, war supplies, and food . . .	12,800		
For presents to the Indians . . .	22,000		
Fire wood for prison guards and prisons . . .	4,000		
For subsistence, remedies, and medicines furnished to the sick in the hospitals . . .	4,200		
Unforeseen expenses . . .	3,000		
For the salaries of the administration . . .	52,838		
For retired officers . . .	7,300		
For pay of companies of soldiers . . .	154,812		
For wages and maintenance of employees of stores and offices in Colony . . .	15,161		
For rental of stores and offices . . .	4,425		
For ordinary allowances . . .	4,470		
For extraordinary allowances . . .	5,433	6	8

	l	s	d
For other divers expenses . . .	22,196	17	

* * *

	l	s	d
For fortifications and reparations . . .	82,457		

* * *

For the maintenance of fortifications and civil establishments . . .	12,000		
For the expenses of Fort St. Frederic . . .	49,051	12	5
Additional funds supplied from receipts from the [Domaine d'Occident]*	262,833	5	10

* * *

Total of funds provided . . .	746,177	2	11

Expenditures

For the construction and maintenance of boats and canoes . . .	5,053	5	
For voyages . . .	7,565	15	
For freight of foodstuff . . .	21,392	4	9
Labour costs . . .	20,641	7	8

---

* The Domaine d'Occident was the administrative unit of New France charged with receiving the King's income from import and export duties, seigniorial charges, and returns from the monopolies of the state.

	l	*s*	*d*
For purchase of merchandise, war supplies, and food . . .	318,253	5	11
For purchase of fire wood . . .	13,355	3	7
For hospitals . . .	6,084	6	4
For unforeseen expenses . . .	13,490	2	2
For salaries of the administration . . .	52,838		
For retired officers . . .	7,300		
For pay of companies of soldiers . . .	148,240		
For wages and maintenance of employees of stores and offices in Colony . . .	24,310	15	
For rental of houses and offices . . .	4,500		
For ordinary allowances . . .	4,470		
For extraordinary allowances . . .	5,433	6	8
For other divers expenses . . .	20,534	7	
Fortifications and reparations . . .	21,569	9	7
For artillery . . .	1,014	2	

*   *   *

Balance

The funds provided to be drawn on the King's budget and from additional funds totalled . . .	746,177	2	11
The expenses . . . for the year 1743 . . .	859,052	11	8
. . . the expenses exceeded the receipts by . . .	112,875	8	9

BIGOT

Done at Quebec, October 15, 1748.

*141. "BEAUHARNOIS AND HOCQUART TO THE MINISTER, CANADA, OCTOBER 25, 1729" (P.A.C., C 11 A, Vol. 51, f. 15).

. . . The Sieur de Silly made an arrangement with the Sieur Gatin, a merchant of this city, to send two workers this summer, at the King's expense, in case the slate was not good, but as it was found to be of good quality His Majesty was not obliged to assume the expenses of these workers. . . . The Sieur de Sarazin, on whose seigniory is found this slate quarry, is working at forming a company for its exploitation and it will be requested of you, Monseigneur, that you give free passage to workers on the King's vessel next year.

*   *   *

We have accounted to His Majesty . . . of the progress in the commerce of building timbers which we send from Canada to the Islands. . . . A ship . . . was sent this year loaded with 3,500 planks. . . .

It is certain that the Canadians will undertake the construction of . . . ships as soon as men, and specially workers, are available, but labour costs are too dear in this country where workers are paid 3 livres a day to expect a great enough profit from the sale of ships. . . .

*142. "HOCQUART TO THE MINISTER, QUEBEC, OCTOBER 29, 1740" (P.A.C., C 11 A, Vol. 73, f. 301).

. . . I have had prepared, in the prescribed format, a statement of the commerce of the colony. Imports totalled 2,053,581 l., 15s., 1d.; exports and letters of exchange totalled 2,222,718 l., 12s. Exports exceeded imports by 167,136 l., 16s., 11d., a considerable enough amount in which, nevertheless, it must be observed, was included in the exports, by error, the sum of 136,000 livres, this being the cost of the 8 ships constructed. This sum would be justly included if all these ships had been constructed and equipped at the expense of the merchants of France. There were but two that were so . . . evaluated at 19,000 livres . . . therefore, there must be deducted from the exports the sum of 117,000 livres which reduces the surplus to . . . 50,136 l., 16s., 11d.

There are certainly some parts of the commerce of the colony which are not included. . . . Should it please you to compare the . . . commerce of the year 1739 to that of 1738, you will find a great difference . . . The expenditures on His Majesty's behalf, the constructions of individuals, the fishing establishments, the iron, tobacco, and principally the wheat, biscuits, and other food supplies had a greater consumption and consequently increased commerce.

*143. "HOCQUART TO THE MINISTER, QUEBEC, OCTOBER 31, 1742" (P.A.C., C 11 A, Vol. 78, f. 166).

I have the honour to send you the statement of yearly expenses for the construction and equipment of the war ship *Le Canada* . . . from 1738 until its departure in the month of April last. These expenses total, according to the general summary that I made, . . . 217,707 l., 12s., 4d. . . .

*144. "ST. MAURICE FORGES IN CANADA, QUEBEC, SEPTEMBER 30, 1740" (P.A.C., C 11 A, Vol. 111-2, f. 81-85).

To the Intendant:

The establishment of these forges was made with the general welfare of the Colony in mind. . . . The establishments could not have been made without the considerable advances made by the King to the Company formed according to the project submitted by M. Olivier, who came [to Canada] in 1735, having been sent for this purpose by . . . Maurepas.

The work was begun in 1736 — all the primary works were made under the direction of the said Olivier — but having found that much more work was entailed than had been foreseen, and having been deceived by the workers employed in the erection of the first buildings, added to which there were a large number of set-backs and difficulties, which occasioned much expenses, he spent 200,000 livres more than had been estimated for his project. . . . The Company, after spending the advances provided by His Majesty, found that to complete the establishment and to maintain it, was obliged to contract debts the payment of which is today difficult. . . .

The year 1738 was the first year of operation. . . . Only a little iron was produced, for the blacksmiths that the Sieur Simonet . . . had brought from France in 1737 were hard to control; a few, such as the foreman, did not know their trade, and others were unruly.

In 1739 it was necessary to build a second forge which was not finished until this year, 1740. . . .

. . . Olivier went to France last year . . . to report on his establishment. His trip furnished the occasion . . . to bring back . . . workers . . . which again increased the expense . . .

During his absence many of the buildings and works which had been badly constructed were repaired. This new expense was very heavy. I will not speak of the many other causes leading to expenses which a more experienced forge foreman . . . would have avoided.

TASCHEREAU [AGENT OF THE MARINE TREASURY]

*145. "ST. MAURICE FORGES IN CANADA, QUEBEC, OCTOBER 25, 1742" (P.A.C., C 11 A, Vol. 112-2, f. 22-38).

To the Minister of Marine:

We have received the letter . . . which you wrote us the 27 April last concerning the St. Maurice Forges. . . .

The Sieur Estebe was not prepared to submit a statement to M. Hocquart until a few days ago. It is after examining this statement that we have prepared the attached memoir which will permit you, Monseigneur, to judge the worth of the establishment and . . . we have added a few of our reflections. . . .

*   *   *

... a profit of 13,640 livres, 10 deniers will never influence a Company to take over . . . such an establishment because of the large sums that must be reimbursed . . . : these consist of 192,642 livres, 6 sous, 7 deniers . . . advanced by His Majesty, and another sum of about 160,000 livres . . . the excess of expenditures over profits since their establishment until October 1, 1740, is 390,883 livres, 5 deniers, from which should be deducted the sum of 39,184 livres, 8 sous, 11 deniers due . . . ; this deduction made the total excess of expenses over profits 350 to 360 thousand livres. . . .

* * *

In default of finding a Company [to undertake the management of the Forges] the other alternatives are:

1—to exploit . . . the Forges in the King's name.

2—or abandon them completely, or finally, to find some new advantages for the formation of a new Company which would convince them to undertake the enterprise.

HOCQUART

*146. "ST. MAURICE FORGES, GENERAL INVENTORY, FEBRUARY 12, 1746" (P.A.C., C 11 A, Vol. 112-2, f. 180-206).

To Hocquart:

	livres	sous	deniers
Church ornaments	1,352	15	
Tools, etc.	205	5	
Furnaces, etc.	30,697	15	5
Forges	50,640	17	9
Moulds	644	10	
Furnishings	1,979	4	
Livestock	3,584		
Munitions, merchandise	60,253	10	10
Wood	551	11	
Planks	2,330		
Buildings, houses	46,979	16	2
Sheds	859	10	
Roads, bridges, etc.	4,983	8	
	205,062	3	2

ESTEBE AND DE L'ISLE

Done at the St. Maurice Forges, February 12, 1746.

147. "PETER KALM AT THREE RIVERS, 1749"
(Kalm, *Travels*, Vol. 2, pp. 249-51).

Whilst my company was resting, I went on horseback to view the iron-works. The country which I passed through was pretty high, sandy, and generally flat. I saw neither stones nor mountains here.

The iron-works, which is the only one in this country, lies three miles to the west of Trois Rivières. Here are two great forges, besides two lesser ones to each of the great ones, and under the same roof with them. The bellows were made of wood, and everything else, as it is in the Swedish forges. The melting ovens stand close to the forges, and are the same as ours. The ore is got two French miles and a half from the iron-works, and is carried thither on sledges.

*   *   *

The ore is pretty rich and lies in loose lumps in the veins, of the size of two fists. . . . These lumps are full of holes, which are filled with ochre. The ore is so soft that it may be crushed betwixt the fingers . . .

Charcoals are to be had in great abundance here, because all the country round this place is covered with woods. . . . The iron which is here made, was to me described as soft, pliable, and tough, and is said to have the quality of not being attacked by rust so early as other iron; . . . This iron-work was first founded in 1733 by private persons, who afterwards ceded it to the King; they cast cannon and mortars here, . . . iron stoves, . . . kettles . . . , not to mention the bars which are made here. . . . It is agreed on all hands that the revenues of the iron-works do not pay the expenses which the King must every year be at in maintaining it. They lay the fault on the bad state of the population, and say that the few inhabitants have enough to do with agriculture, and that it therefore costs great trouble and large sums, to get a sufficient number of workmen. But however plausible this may appear, yet it is surprising that the King should be a loser in carrying on this work; for the ore is easily broken, very near the iron-work, and very fusible. The iron is good, and can be very conveniently dispersed over the country. This is moreover the only iron-work in the country, from which everybody must supply himself with iron tools, and what other iron he wants. But the officers and servants belonging to the iron-work appear to be in very affluent circumstances.

C

THE CANADIENS

There are not too many extended characterizations of the Canadiens of New France. Here and there, and by bits and pieces, it is possible to form some opinion of their general chartacteristics. The three following documents, written between 1721 and 1749, indicate somewhat the current opinions on the inhabitants of New France. All three are from the pens of foreigners: two Frenchmen and a Swede. All recognize one thing clearly and that is the existence of a different culture—one that may be justifiably called *Canadien*.

Pierre François Xavier de Charlevoix was a French Jesuit who visited the length and breadth of the French possessions in North America. His *Histoire de la Nouvelle France*, first published in 1744, well reflects the contemporary outlook of a well-educated citizen of France. His view of New France and its inhabitants will be found in Document 148.

The second characterization, Document 149, is from the pen of Gilles Hocquart. He had been intendant of New France since 1729 and devoted his not inconsiderable energies to the well-being of the colony. His characterization was a little condescending, as befits a metropolitan, but was probably judicious.

The Swedish naturalist Peter Kalm also left an assessment of the Canadiens, which is presented in Document 150. The introduction to the English translation is also included, for it reflects a pardonable English pride and prejudice.

*148. "CHARLEVOIX ON THE CANADIANS" (Charlevoix, *Histoire de la Nouvelle France*, Vol. 5, pp. 117-18, 252-54).

* * *

I have already said that there are but 7,000 souls at Quebec, but one finds a choice little world from which nothing is missing to form a pleasant society. A Governor-General . . . , a nobility . . . , officers . . . , an Intendant . . . , a Superior Council . . . , a Marine Commissioner . . . , a Chief Magistrate . . . , a Master of the Roads . . . , a Grand Master of the Woods and Forests, whose jurisdiction is surely the largest in the Universe; affluent merchants or those living as if they were; a Bishop

..., Seminary ..., Recollets ..., Jesuits; three Communities of Women
..., circles as brilliant as anywhere at the house of the wife of the
Governor and at that of the wife of the Intendant. This, it seems to me,
provides all the people necessary to pass the time agreeably.

* * *

... One does not see in this country people who are rich, and this is
unfortunate, for they like to display, and almost no one amuses himself
by hoarding. They set a good table if they are able ... ; if not, then
they retrench on food so as to be able to be well-dressed. ...

* * *

... Everyone here has the necessities of life: little is paid to the King;
the *habitant* does not know the *taille*;* bread is to be had at a fair price;
meat and fish are not expensive, but wine and cloth and all that must
come from France is costly. Those who complain the most of the cost
are the *gentilhommes* and the officers. ... Usually the women's dowry is
but much spirit, companionship, agreeableness, and a great fecundity.
...

... The world does not know a more healthful climate ... no particular diseases ravage the country, the countryside and the woods are filled
with marvellous medicinal plants, and the trees provide balms of great
virtue. These advantages should at least retain here those that Providence graced by birth in the country, but the imprudence, aversion to
assiduous work, lack of discipline, and spirit of independence have
always led to a loss of many young people and this has retarded the
growth of the Colony.

*149. "MEMOIR TO THE MINISTER CONTAINING A CHARACTER-
IZATION OF THE FRENCH-CANADIAN POPULATION, NOVEM-
BER 8, 1737" (Munro, *Seigniorial Documents*, pp.
185-88).

The population of the colony of New France is about 40,000 people
of all ages and sex among which there are 10,000 men capable of bearing
arms. The Canadians are husky, well built, and of a vigorous tempera-
ment. As trades are not dominated by specialization, and since, at the
establishment of the colony, tradesmen were rare, necessity has made
them ingenious from generation to generation. The rural inhabitants
handle the axe very adroitly. They make themselves most of the tools
and utensils needed for farming, and build their own houses and barns.
Many are weavers and make linen, and a large cloth which is called
droguet which they use to clothe themselves and their families.

---

* A tax on farmers in France.

They love honours and praise, and pride themselves on their courage, and are extremely sensitive to criticism and the least punishment. They are self-seeking, vindictive, subject to drunkenness, make much use of liquor, and are not the most truthful people.

This characterization suits the majority, especially the rural inhabitants. Those in the cities have fewer faults. All are attached to religion. One sees few perfidious people. They are fickle, and have too high an opinion of themselves, which lessens their abilities to succeed in trade, agriculture, and commerce. Add to this the idleness occasioned by the long and rigorous winters. They love hunting, sailing, and travelling and are not as gross and rustic as our peasants of France. They are amenable enough when we flatter them and govern them with justice, but are by nature indocile.

It is more and more necessary to establish the respect due to authority especially amongst the people of the countryside. This aspect of administration has always been most important and the most difficult to implement. One means of achieving this is to choose the officers of the administration for the countryside from amongst the inhabitants who are wise and capable of commanding, and to give all the attention possible to supporting their authority. It can be said that a lack of firmness by the governments in the past has contributed to insubordination. For several years now crimes have been punished, disorders have been checked by suitable chastisements. Policing of public roads, cabarets, etc., has been better, and in general, the inhabitants have been controlled better than in the past. There are few noble families in Canada, but they are so large that there are many gentlemen.

Here are the names of the principal families:

Families	Branches
Le Gardeur . . .	Repentigny Croisille Tilly and Beauvais St. Pierre
Denys . . .	Denys de la Ronde Bonaventure
D'Ailleboust . . .	de St. Simon Périgny Menthet Dargenteuil Des Musseaux
Boucher . . .	This family is established at Boucherville near Montreal; the eldest, who is nearly 90 years old, has more than 150 children, grandchildren, brothers, nephews, grandnephews.

Contrecoeur . . .	All these families are descendants of the
La Valterie . . .	soldiers of the Carignan regiment sent to
St. Ours . . .	Canada in 1665.
Meloisses . . .	
Tarieu de la Pérade	
Aubert (de la Chesnaye . . .)	
Hertel . . .	These two families are very numerous.
Godefoy . . .	
Damour . . .	

There are other gentlemen who serve in the troops, but the families have not been as long established in the country.

All the gentlemen, children of officers, wish to enter the services, which is praiseworthy in itself, but as most of them are poor they join but to receive the King's money rather than for any other reason. The Governor-General chooses from amongst the best candidates. We have trouble convincing the others that they should develop their lands. Perhaps it would be advisable to send a few to France to serve in the navy so that the nobility and better classes of the country may be more devoted to France.

(ATTRIBUTED TO HOCQUART)

150. "PETER KALM ON THE CANADIANS, 1749"
(Kalm, *Voyages*, Vol. 2, pp. iii, 224-25, 227).

"Preface of the Editor"

I could have left this volume without preface, was it not for some circumstances which I am going to mention.

The author of this account of *North America* is a *Swede*, and therefore seems always to shew a peculiar way of thinking in regard to the *English* in general, and in regard to the first proprietors and inhabitants of *Philadelphia* in particular. The *French*, the natural enemies of the *English*, have, for upwards of a century, been the allies of the *Swedes*, who therefore are in general more fond of them than of the *English*. The external politeness of the *French* in *Canada* fully captivated our author, prejudiced him in their favour, and alienated his mind, though injustly, from the *English*. I have therefore now and then, in remarks, been obliged to do the English justice, especially when I saw the author carried away either by prejudice or misinformation. [Preface.]

MONTREAL

The difference between the manners and customs of the French in Montreal and Canada, and those of the English in the American colonies, is as great as that between the manners of those two nations in Europe. The women in general are handsome here; they are well bred, and virtuous, with an innocent and becoming freedom. They dress out very fine on Sundays; and though on the other days they do not take much pains with other parts of their dress, yet they are very fond of adorning their heads, the hair of which is always curled and powdered and orna- mented with glittering bodkins and aigrettes. Every day but Sunday, they wear a little neat jacket, and a short petticoat which hardly reaches half the leg, and in this particular they seem to the Indian women. The heels of their shoes are high, and very narrow, and it is surprising how they walk on them. In their knowledge of economy, they greatly surpass the English women in the plantations, who indeed have taken the liberty of throwing all the burthen of housekeeping upon their husbands, and sit in their chairs all day with folded arms. The women in Canada on the contrary do not spare themselves, especially among the common people. . . . However, they seem rather remiss in regard to the cleaning of utensils, and apartments; for sometimes the floors, both in the town and in the country, were hardly cleaned once in six months, which is a disagreeable sight to one who comes from amongst the Dutch and English, where the constant scouring and scrubbing of floors, is reckoned as important as the exercise of religion itself. . . .

The men are extremely civil, and take their hats off to every person indifferently, whom they meet in the streets. It is customary to return a visit the day after you have received one. . . .

*   *   *

Mechanics, such as architecture, cabinet-work, turning, and the like, were not yet so forward here as they ought to be; and the English in that particular, out-do the French. The chief cause of this is, that scarce any other people than dismissed soldiers come to settle here, who have not had any opportunity of learning a mechanical trade, but have some- times accidentally, and through necessity, been obliged to it. . . .

D

THE CHURCH

The functions of the Church in Canadian society were established in 1663 when the pioneer and missionary Church of New France was replaced by one concerned primarily with the needs of the Canadians rather than those of the Indians. At the same time the supremacy of secular institutions was established. The creation of the See of Quebec in 1674, and France's role in the choice of a bishop, are evidence of the Gallican nature of the Canadian Church.

The first document concerns the funds available to the Church for the fulfillment of its tasks. It also lists the administrative divisions, and the religious orders, which served Canada. From these incomes the costs of the clerical functions in the colony were met: administration, education, medical services, pensions for aged clerics, and all other expenses incidental to the completion of their mission.

The next two documents, concerning the tithe, should be related to the tasks which the Church was expected to fulfill. If the Church was insistent upon the collection of its dues it was not from purely mercenary motives, but rather because of all its real needs.

A further illustration of this, and of the social role of the Church in New France, may be gathered from Documents 154 and 155. Hospitals were not a money-making proposition. The solution, then as now, was an appeal to the State for financial assistance.

The last document, 157, relates the events which took place after the death of the second Bishop of Quebec, Monseigneur de Saint-Vallier. The rather amusing, and perhaps deplorable moves and counter-moves, however, represent some of the tensions and social conflicts of New France in this period. The intendant, Dupuy, supported by some members of the Superior Council, tried to impose his choice as the interim head of the Canadian Church. The governor, allied with an opposing faction, tried to enforce his choice until such time as a new bishop was appointed. At the same time as the secular leaders opposed each other, the conflict took on an inter-church aspect in that the Canadian clergy opposed the French clergy. The resolution of the problem was that Dupuy was recalled, the governor was admonished, the Superior Council's powers were further restricted, and a new bishop was appointed. However, the appointee, Monseigneur Louis François Duplessis de Mornay, although bishop from 1727 to 1733, never came to New France, but ruled his See through a coadjutor.

*151. "MEMOIR ON THE ESTATE OF THE BISHOP, THE CHAPTER AND OTHER RELIGIOUS COMMUNITIES OF CANADA (BETWEEN 1724 AND 1727)" (*Mandements des Évêques*, Vol. 1, pp. 514-22).

THE SEE OF QUEBEC

The revenue of the See of Quebec is between 9,000 and 10,000 livres
. . . from three abbeys. . . . In addition the palace at Quebec and 500
livres Canadian money that the . . . concessioners give to assist in the
payment of import duties. The Bishop is the recipient of 4,000 livres
charged to the King's budget for the support of cures, priests of the
seminary, and the construction of churches. The total of the revenues
may amount to 5,000 and a few livres.

THE CHAPTER

The revenue of the Chapter consists of about . . . 4,500 livres . . . of
which only 2,000 is drawn because of retired clerics. There is besides a
holding in Canada called *la Petite Nation* which, as yet, produces no
income. . . .

PARISH OF QUEBEC

The revenue of the Parish of Quebec is drawn from the past budget
of the King . . . and is 1,000 livres of France plus the revenue of the
church benches, a few lands, and a few endowments . . . , collections, and
burials. All together these total 3,000 livres.

SEMINARY OF QUEBEC

The revenue of the Seminary of Foreign Missions established at Quebec consists of six benefices . . . and in addition income from 2,300
invested by . . . Saint-Vallier, presently Bishop of Quebec, who retains
to himself the interests accruing during his lifetime. . . . In addition the
said Seminary has in the country three well-developed land holdings . . .
which produce yearly . . . 10,000 livres in the money of Canada. The
total income amounts to more than 20,000 livres Canadian. . . .

THE JESUITS

The revenue of . . . the Company of Jesus, of which we know, are,
first, the income derived from the endowment of M. the Commandant of
Sillery, which was 50,000 écus* and the revenue of which is probably
7,500 livres. In addition, from the past budget of the King . . . 5,000
livres for the missions to the Indians and on the new budget of the King,
. . . 1,000. . . . In addition there are many individual endowments . . . ,
several . . . seigniories in Canada of which we do not know the income.
. . . The total of the revenue is more than 20,000 livres of France.

THE RECOLLETS

The . . . Recollets have a 1,200-livres' gratuity from the King's new
budget and their collections. And in addition, an extra gratuity of . . .
500 livres from the new budget. . . .

SEMINARY OF SAINT-SULPICE

The Seminary of Saint-Sulpice at Ville-Marie, seigniors of the Island

---

* An écu was worth three livres.

of Montreal, have the whole Island as a seigniory which produces 1,000
écus in income. In addition the revenues of the city . . . plus 200 écus
on the King's new budget. . . . The total is about 9 to 10,000 livres. . . .

THE NURSING SISTERS OF MONTREAL

They have lost the income from their endowment which was 20,000
livres that Madame de Bullion had given them, but was included in the
estate of Monsieur de la Dauversière at his death, and which the King
seized. Monsieur Macé gave an endowment . . . which produces 950
livres, and from . . . le baron de Fancamp, and several other benefactors
. . . 633 livres. . . . And from the King's new budget 1,000 livres. They
owe a considerable sum for the buildings that they have had to construct
and for which they must find the means to pay. The total of their revenue
is about 5,000 livres.

L'HÔTEL DIEU DE MONTREAL

. . . The total of the revenue of the Hotel Dieu of Ville-Marie is, or
can be, about 1,000 écus.

SISTERS OF THE CONGREGATION

. . . The total of their assured revenue is about 1,000 livres and with
the present gratuities, about 4,000 livres.

NURSING SISTERS OF QUEBEC

. . . The total of their revenue is about 6,000 livres but this must
be increased.

* * *

RELIGIOUS INSTITUTES TO BE SUPPORTED

See of Quebec, Chapter of Quebec, Parish of Quebec, Seminary of
Quebec, Jesuits, Recollets, Seminary of Saint-Sulpice, Nursing Sisters of
Montreal, Hôtel Dieu of Montreal, Sisters of the Congregation, Parish
of Ville-Marie, Nursing Sisters of Quebec, Hôtel Dieu of Quebec, Ursulines, Cures of Canada, General Hospital.

* * *

*152. "JUDGMENT WHICH, AT THE REQUEST OF THE DEACON OF
STE. FOYE, CONDEMNS EIGHT INHABITANTS TO PAY THE
TITHES . . . QUEBEC, MARCH 27, 1713" (*Ordonnances et
Jugements*, Vol. 3, pp. 158-59).

Michel Bégon . . . , Intendant of justice, police, and finance in New
France . . .
The Sieur Louis Gaultier, captain of the militia of the seigniory of
Cap Rouge, and deacon of the parish of Notre-Dame-de-Foye, has rep-

resented that . . . LeBrun, Jesuit . . . has been refused the tithes due for the . . . year 1712. . . .

We condemn the said Grégoire . . . Durbois, widow Petitclair . . . to pay to the Sieur Gaultier the tithes which they owe. . . .

BÉGON

*153. "DIRECTIVE ON THE REFUSAL OF ABSOLUTION TO THOSE WHO REFUSE TO PAY THE TITHE, APRIL 1717" (*Mandements des Évêques*, Vol. 1, pp. 491-92).

* * *

We have lamented, since we were established as pastor of this diocese, My Dearly Beloved Brethren in Our Lord, the inveterate, and almost irremediable abuses of a large number of our parishioners, who easily persuade themselves that they may approach the Sacraments with surety, and not pay their tithes, or but paying a part of them and often with the worst of their wheat, and paying it at the time and in the manner that they judge convenient without any regard for the obligation which they have to pay it all and from the choicest wheat at Easter time as is provided for in the ritual. For this reason, fearing that God may impute to you the negligence of most of the inhabitants of your parishes . . . we continue to assure you that it is our intention that you hold firm to . . . an interrogation of the penitents . . . on the tithes, and to refuse benediction and absolution if they have not satisfied the requirements.

JEAN

*154. "LETTER TO THE PRESIDENT OF THE MARINE COUNCIL, MARCH 2, 1748" (*R.A.P.Q.*, 1935-36, pp. 287-89).

As you probably know . . . , the Hospital of Montreal was established by King's patent . . . in April 1694 and was administered until October 14 last by Hospitalers known as the Charon Brothers who, as early as October 9, 1745, had presented a request that they be relieved of the charge of the . . . hospital because of their small numbers. . . .

As a consequence of which . . . an ordonnance was issued by the Sovereign Council of Quebec relieving the Hospitalers . . . and provisionally naming Madame D'Youville, a widow of an . . . officer, who, since the death of her husband, apparently joined a secular community in order to care for the said hospital. . . . And she has managed and administered the revenues, in conformity with the manner . . . prescribed by the ordonnance . . . which I forward, also a power of attorney of the same date addressed to myself . . . permitting me to treat with the creditors of the said hospital, who have placed a seizure on an income of 800 livres due to the hospital. . . .

L'ABBÉ DE L'ISLE DIEU

*155. "TABLE OF THE PRESENT DEBTS OF THE HOSPITAL OF MONT-REAL OWED TO CREDITORS WHO ARE IN FRANCE, PARIS, MAY 24, 1752" *(R.A.P.Q.*, 1935-1936, pp. 351-52).

According to the deposition of creditors . . . filed April 17, 1728, and the decrees of the Superior Council of Quebec rendered . . . July 29, 1735, the debts of the said hospital were fixed at:

	livres	*sous*	*deniers*
Debts	24,940	13	9
Costs	587	11	
Total of said debts as of July 29, 1735	25,528	4	9
Payments to creditors prior to 1750 reduced the debt to	19,776	11	3
On July 29, 1750 the sum of was distributed to creditors	2,729	6	
Present balance due	17,047	6	3
Income due	1,573	15	
Balance due	15,473	11	3

*   *   *

L'ABBÉ DE L'ISLE DIEU
*Representative of the
Bishop of Quebec at Paris*

*156. "ORDONNANCE PROHIBITING THE INHABITANTS TO GALLOP THEIR HORSES ON LEAVING CHURCH, FEBRUARY 29, 1716" *(Arrêts et Règlements,* Vol. 2, p. 286).

We prohibit . . . all persons, in carioles as well as on horseback, to trot or gallop their horses on leaving church . . . under penalty of a fine of 20 livres. . . .

BÉGON

*157. "REPORT OF M. DUPUY, INTENDANT, ON THE TROUBLES WHICH OCCURRED AT QUEBEC IN 1727 AND 1728 AFTER

THE DEATH OF MONSEIGNEUR DE SAINT-VALLIER, BISHOP
OF QUEBEC" (*R.A.P.Q.*, 1920-1921, pp. 78-105).

It is very important that the King remedy promptly the disorders
which have occurred in Canada since the death of the Bishop of Quebec.
The reports made in France by the deputy of the Chapter are so odious,
so filled with impostures and calumnies against . . . those who are in
power and who have had to bring order . . . for the maintenance of
justice and the authority of the King. . . .

Saint-Vallier had made his will and requested burial in the parish
church of his General Hospital where, for a number of years, he had
retired. . . .

Immediately after his death I placed a seal on his belongings. Two
deputies of the Chapter of Quebec presented themselves demanding that
I not pledge the seals and registers of the diocese in that, by the death
of the Bishop, the jurisdiction over the diocese devolved to the Chapter. . . .

. . . The canons of Quebec dared to invent and spread in France the
odious claim that I had the Bishop buried by children of the hang-
man. . . .

He was buried with all due solemnity, and with all offices, in the
presence of all priests, Jesuits, and Recollets, present at the General
Hospital, in the presence of members of the judiciary, of the people of this
parish, and the poor of the hospital, each of whom had a tallow in his
hand. . . .

The canons . . . rang the alarm bell of the cathedral, sounded a general
alert, and informed the city that the hospital was on fire . . . ; the Canons
used their prestige to convince the more simple-minded, and led these
on the pretext of a fire, to the General-Hospital.

. . . I thanked the people for their zeal . . . assuring them that there
was no fire . . .

As for the canons, they entered the Church tumultuously and knocked
down the people who were praying by the tomb of the Bishop. They
tried twice to remove the Holy Host. They deposed the superior of the
hospital . . . they placed the church under an interdict. . . .

Can there be anything more indecent or absurd than to interdict a
church because the Bishop is buried there? Can there be anything more
irreligious or inhuman than to interdict . . . the administration of the
sacraments in a hospital where there are people dying every day?

*   *   *

DUPUY

E

THE CONQUEST OF CANADA

The period 1713 to 1748 has been characterized as one of relative peace. There was but one actual war in America: King George's War, the American name for the War of the Austrian Succession of 1740-48. New England troops commanded by Sir William Pepperell captured Louisbourg in 1745, but, by the Treaty of Aix-la-Chapelle of 1748, the fortress was returned to the French, much to the disgust of the New Englanders.

However, the years from 1713 to the outbreak of the French and Indian War which began in 1754, three years before the declaration of the Seven Years' War, were filled with strife and skirmishes. The Canadian and French response to the loss of Acadia was the construction of Louisbourg. At the same time, the Indians were incited to attack the New Englanders in the 1720's. Both sides offered premiums for all male enemy scalps turned in. In 1749, at a time when a peace existed between the Crowns of Great Britain and France, the English founded Halifax. In the following year the rivals both established forts on the Bay of Fundy.

The Canadians also fortified the traditional Champlain-Richelieu invasion route. The Canadians built Fort St. Frederic at Crown Point in 1731 and Ticonderoga in 1755. The New Yorkers countered by building Forts Edward and William Henry.

To the South-west the Canadian and French strategy involved containing the British-Americans behind the Appalachian Mountains. In the far South the founding of New Orleans in 1718, and the incorporation of the native tribes into an alliance system, provided a barrier. The Louisiana-New France link was not merely one of communications, strategy, and a common metropolis, but was further bound by the choice of two Canadians as governors of Louisiana: de Bienville Le Moyne and the second Vaudreuil.

In the West, along the line of the Great Lakes, both sides thrust and parried. The Canadians established Fort Niagara in 1720; the New Yorkers built Oswego in 1721. In 1749, the same year as the founding of Halifax, Fort Rouillé was built on the north shore of Lake Ontario. A little later its name was changed to Toronto. South of the Lakes, the area known as the Upper Mississippi and the Ohio Valley, was laced by forts.

Perhaps one of the most amazing features of this period of Canadian history is that New France, which only had a population of about 55,000 as against the 1,500,000 or so British-Americans, was able to encompass, and control, so much of the continent. The results of the Canadian Continental strategy were to bar the British-Americans from the interior. The success of the *Canadiens* helped to precipitate the French and Indian War in 1754, when a military expedition led by a British-American officer called George Washington attempted to assert British claims in the Ohio Valley. Washington's failure was followed by that of Braddock in 1755 who gallantly (he took his mistress along) though foolishly led his brightly-uniformed troops through the green forests, very much against the advice of the British-Americans. Braddock's army was severely defeated. The War of the Conquest had begun.

The War may be divided into two phases. From 1754 to 1758 the French and Canadians were on the offensive, and were, on the whole successful in their military endeavours. The capture of Louisbourg in 1758 and the successes of the English and British-Americans in the South and West from that date until the Capitulation of Montreal in 1760 were the second phase.

In this crisis period of the history of New France, survival, more than ever, depended upon maintaining communications with the metropolis, and the unification of all elements of Canadian society to meet the foe. The first requisite was beyond the control of the colony, and the failure of France to fully appreciate the significance of the war in America resulted in too little aid being sent too late.

In New France, Canadian society was rent by quarrels between the Canadian-born governor Pierre de Rigaud, Marquis de Vaudreuil-Cavagnal, who had been appointed in 1755, and Louis Joseph, Marquis de Montcalm, the French general named to head military affairs in Canada in 1756. The already critical situation was further troubled by the financial depredations of the intendant, François Bigot, and his coterie of corrupt favourites.

The cold war on the eastern front is described in Document 159. The French viewed the founding of Halifax, quite properly, as an aggressive act. The following selection, 160, is a Canadian's views on the European versus the Canadian concepts of strategy. The same year, 1755, was notable for the expulsion of the Acadians, and the Pastoral Letter of the Bishop, Document 161, vividly presents the climate of public opinion.

The Vaudreuil-Montcalm-Bigot triangle is the subject-matter of

Documents 162 to 170. The conflict of personalities, strategy, and the rumours of corruption combined with insufficient French aid, and the superiority of the forces of the enemy, sealed New France's fate.

The "Memoir On Canada" which follows is similar to the writings of La Hontan presented earlier. The ultimate consequences of the loss to France of its American possessions is considered, and the future results envisioned indicate a noteworthy prescience.

The results of the Battle of the Plains of Abraham are presented in the last three documents. Vaudreuil, immediately after the battle, initiated the controversy over the strategy of the battle, and affirmed that he would not cede the colony. In the following year, although Lévis won the battle of Sainte-Foy, continued English naval superiority limited the possibility of aid from France, and Montreal capitulated. The French Régime in Canada was at an end.

*158. "LA GALISSIONIÈRE TO MINISTER, QUEBEC, NOVEMBER 6, 1747" (*Collection de Memoires,* Vol. 3, 399-400)

Your letters on the treaties frightened me. The abandonment of so useful . . . a colony is unbelievable. I am sure you will not consent to them. The letters bind my arms. I would have been able, this winter, to undertake a few endeavours on the Hudson's Bay . . . and a few other posts. War is never made without expenses. . . .

It will always be essential to have a large detachment in Acadia; it will surely cost dear. . . . Inaction saves nothing. If we do not attack we will be attacked and the expenses of defensive actions will exceed those of offensive ones.

. . . Let us put ourselves in a state to carry the war to the enemy: it is the only way to assure security here.

*159. "MINISTER TO LAJONQUIÈRE, VERSAILLES, SEPTEMBER 11, 1750" (P.A.C., Series B, Vol. 91, f. 298-300).

I informed the King of the contents of the two letters you wrote me. . . .

. . . One concerns your correspondence with . . . Cornwallis, governor of Acadia. . . .

There is no doubt that the last letter that this Governor wrote to you on the 5 of May was very indecent in all ways; and we cannot doubt that it will be disapproved of by the Court of England. But it should be admitted that yours of April 2, to which his letter was an answer, was, on the whole, too biting relative to the letters he had sent you previously. . . .

* * *

. . . the worrisome and enterprising character of . . . Cornwallis, Governor of Acadia, which has manifested itself on all occasions, especially in the enterprise he attempted in the first days of May, leads one to fear that he may attempt new ones to capture by force the post on the St. John River, and that of Pecoudy.

* * *

If the English General attempts new enterprises against these posts, or any others which the French possess that are not in the peninsula of Acadia, it is His Majesty's intention that you represent to the Commander of the English troops that peace having been happily established . . . it has been agreed by the Treaty of Aix-la-Chapelle that all possessions would be reciprocally returned on the basis which they were before the war. . . .

The attached letter will explain the King's intentions on the conduct you must follow with regards to the enterprises of . . . Cornwallis. . . . I have two observations to add. . . .

The first is that in the present circumstances there is nothing of greater importance than to maintain the Indians in their present dispositions. His Majesty permits you to make the gifts that you judge necessary, but at the same time he desires that you take measures to ensure that there will be no abuses in the distribution. . . .

The second is that if, on the pretext that the clause of the treaty of peace providing that pre-war possessions and conditions be re-established . . . the English demand that you evacuate the detachments from the St. John River and those of Pecoudy, you will answer that it is precisely because Cornwallis contravened the clause in attempting to force the inhabitants of those areas to take an oath of loyalty to England that you and . . . de la Galissionière found yourselves constrained to take the precaution of sending these detachments to those Frenchmen who requested protection against the menaces of the English General.

*160. "VAUDREUIL TO THE MINISTER OF MARINE, MONTREAL, OCTOBER 30, 1755" (Casgrain, *Extraits*, p. 109).

* * *

I must, Monseigneur, . . . represent to you that it is not necessary that there be a General to command these battalions. We can, without him, discipline and manoeuvre them. The wars in this country are very different from those of Europe. We must proceed with much prudence and thus run fewer risks. We have few people and the loss of a few is greatly felt.

No matter how brave the commander of the troops may be, he cannot know the country. He would, perhaps, not follow the advice given to him by subaltern officers. He would make up his own mind or take the advice of misinformed people. . . . I base my representation on the results of the campaign of M. de Dieskau. Besides which, I would not hide from you, Monseigneur, the fact that the Canadians and the Indians would not march with as great confidence under the command of an officer from France as under an officer of this colony. I hope that you will agree with my presentations. They have no other end than the service and well-being of the colony.

*161. "PASTORAL LETTER RE PUBLIC PRAYERS—DISPERSAL OF THE ACADIANS, QUEBEC, FEBRUARY 15, 1756" (*Mandements des Évêques*, Vol. 2, pp. 104-9).

The War which you have supported to date, My Dearly Beloved Brethren, with so much courage, will continue . . . this year, and perhaps with greater intensity than ever. Our enemies, filled with the success they have had down river, and irritated by our victories in the upper part of this colony, are making new preparations and menace us from every side. Their conduct towards the Acadians forewarns us as to what to expect should they be victorious. The Acadians, whose fate can but sadden us, were suddenly disarmed and called together on specious pretexts at different forts. They came unsuspecting and no sooner had they arrived than they were arrested, imprisoned, and then transported to distant and foreign lands. The women, in tears, went into the woods with their children and were exposed to the injuries of the inclement weather and suffered further from want, without help or succour, which harms they preferred to losing their faith. However, the enemy seized a number of them; to intimidate the others, they threatened a form of slavery for their husbands; a few, frightened by this threat, yielded and came to the place of embarkation; the greater number, stripped of everything, took refuge in our lands. The villages are burnt, the churches suffered the same fate, the English sparing only those to be used as prisons for those that could not be embarked. The pastors were seized with violence and expelled forever.

This is, My Dearly Beloved Brethren, the sad condition of Acadia, although the most solemn treaties and the conventions but recently agreed to at the evacuation of Fort Beauséjour appeared to promise a happier fate, which only goes to prove that one cannot rely on all promises no matter how sincere they appear.

H.-M. [PONTBRIAND]

*162. "MEMOIR OF THE KING TO SERVE AS INSTRUCTIONS TO . . .
MONTCALM . . . , VERSAILLES, MARCH 14, 1756"
(Lévis Collection, Vol. 3, pp. 39-41).

*   *   *

The principal object of these operations is the defence of Canada
against the enterprises of the English. His Majesty has given to . . .
Vaudreuil . . . his orders on the use he should make of the troops and
militia within his government for the said defence, as well as other
objects. And, as . . . Montcalm cannot exercise the command that His
Majesty has given him but through the authority of the governor to
whom he is subordinate . . . the Sieur . . . Montcalm will execute . . . all
that he will be ordered to do by the governor-general.

*   *   *

In a word, it will be up to the governor-general to regulate and order
all military operations. . . . Montcalm will be held to the execution of
these orders. He may, however, make any representations that seem
necessary to him . . . But if the governor-general believes that he has
reasons not to defer to the proffered advice . . . Montcalm will obey the
orders . . . without delay.

*163. "DOREIL TO THE MINISTER, QUEBEC, JULY 6, 1755"
(R.A.P.Q., 1944-45, pp. 18-22).

*   *   *

The ration furnished here to a soldier . . . is composed of one and a
half pounds of good bread, four ounces of lard or half a pound of fresh
beef . . . but this is rarely given. There is also a daily ration of dry
beans. On duty or marching, two pounds of bread are given to which
is added two portions of liquor. . . .

*164. "MARQUIS DE VAUDREUIL TO THE CHEVALIER DE LÉVIS,
MONTREAL, SEPTEMBER 16, 1756" *(Lévis Collection,* Vol.
8, p. 39).

*   *   *

. . . I have indicated to M. le Marquis de Montcalm how essential it
is to send a detachment of 1,800 to 2,500 men to attack the enemy . . . *à
la Canadienne.* I hope that circumstances will permit him to do so. . . .

165. "MONTCALM TO MARSHALL DE BELLE ISLE, MONTREAL,
APRIL 12, 1759" (Shortt, *Currency,* Vol. 2, pp. 893-901).

The expenditures which have been paid at Quebec . . . amount to twenty-four millions. The year before, the expenditures amounted to only twelve or thirteen millions. This year they will run up to thirty-six. Everybody appears to be in a hurry to make his fortune before the Colony is lost, which event many, perhaps, may desire as an impenetrable veil over their conduct. The craving after wealth has an influence on the war, and . . . Vaudreuil does not doubt it. Instead of reducing the expenditures of Canada people wish to profit by everything; why abandon positions which serve as a pretext to make private fortunes? Transport is distributed to favourites. The agreement with the contractor is as unknown to me as it is to the public. 'Tis reported that those who have crowded into trade, participate in it. Has the King need of purchasing goods for the Indians? Instead of buying them directly, a favourite is notified who purchases at any price whatever; then M. Bigot has them removed to the King's stores, allowing a profit of one hundred and even one hundred and fifty per cent, to those whom it is desired to favour. Is artillery to be transported, gun-carriages, carts, implements to be made? M. Mercier, commandant of the artillery, is the contractor under other people's names. Everything is badly done and at a high price. This officer, who came out twenty years ago as a simple soldier, will soon be worth about six or seven hundred thousand livres, perhaps a million, if these things continue. I have often respectfully spoken to . . . Vaudreuil and . . . Bigot of these expenses; each throws the blame on his colleague. The people, alarmed at these expenses, fear a depreciation of the paper money of the country: the evil effect is, the cost of food is increasing and the Canadians who do not participate in those illicit profits are disloyal to the Government. . . .

*166. "DOREIL TO THE MINISTER, MONTREAL, OCTOBER 28, 1755"
(*R.A.P.Q.*, 1944-1945, pp. 61-64).

M. de Vaudreuil is far from approving what is going on here. He misses nothing. He has been so frank with me as to go into details and lamented on them. But, I believe, unless there is an explosion things will always be the same. He wants to keep his position, besides which he is forbidden to concern himself with financial matters. . . . He is a leader filled with good intentions, is charitable . . . , easy to approach, and polite . . . , but circumstances, and the present tasks are a little too much for him. He needs an objective counsellor who would keep his spirits up. He appears to treat with me in good faith. I will help him if I can. . . . I would be relieved if the commander who will be sent to us next spring is of a supple and gentle character. He will govern the governor.

167. "VAUDREUIL'S EXCUSES FOR NOT SUPERVISING THE FINANCES, MONTREAL, OCTOBER 15, 1759" (Shortt, *Currency*, Vol. 2, pp. 927-29).

I had the honour to inform you . . . that the existing circumstances did not permit me to take cognizance of the finances, and that I could not do it so long as the war lasted.

* * *

I cannot conceal from you, My Lord, that the Intendant has imparted to me his grief for the suspicions you appear to entertain as to his administration, as appears from the letters he has received from you. He does not deserve them, I am sure. He is full of zeal for the King's service, but as he is rich, or at least passes for such, and as he is a man of merit, the malevolent people are jealous of him and insinuate that the King's finances have contributed to his riches. Intimations of this kind have been made to me against him, but I have good reason to be assured that all he has done is contrary to what people have wished to make me believe, and I see no person who has more at heart the interests of the King or who is a better citizen than he.

* * *

168. "BIGOT TO DE MESSIAC, QUEBEC, AUGUST 13, 1758" (O'Callaghan, *Colonial History of the State of New York*, Vol. 10, pp. 812-13).

I returned from Montreal some days ago; I went there on official business, and at the request of . . . Vaudreuil, whom I found much piqued against . . . Montcalm. He has been informed of a thousand things the army has said of him after the action of the 8th of July, and pretends that . . . Montcalm has been the author of them, having been the first to express them.

. . . Montcalm, on his side, complains that . . . Vaudreuil has no confidence in him, and does not communicate his plans to him. . . .

I am doing my best with the one and the other to induce them to conceal from the public the little reproaches they believe themselves justified in making against one another. . . . A report of a rupture would be as dangerous to the Colony as the entrance of the English army. Too much jealousy has already spread among the different corps.

. . . Montcalm and . . . Vaudreuil are both necessary parties for the preservation and defence of Canada. The former has made himself known as a good General and a man of vast detail, smart and active, zealous for the service. The latter does what he pleases with the Indian Nations and the Canadians, and he is thoroughly conversant with the nature of the fighting in this country; he also knows how to turn to advantage the terror which the English have of the Indians. I am equally attached to both, I should live on the best terms with them, but I doubt if they will do the same; their hauteur is too much opposed the one to the other, and for a long time they have appeared to me to associate only politically.

* * *

*169. "MEMOIR ON THE COMING CAMPAIGN, MARCH 21, 1759"
(*Lévis Collection*, Vol. 4, pp. 144-52).

REFLECTIONS OF . . . MONTCALM
The superior English forces, and the news we have of their preparations all indicate that an all-out attempt will be made to invade Canada. The only area where we can hope that they might not be able to mass in strength, without being too optimistic, is Quebec.
France can, by sending a fleet early, guarantee this area.

COMMENTS OF . . . VAUDREUIL
The reflections of . . . Montcalm on the dangers . . . of an all-out attack on the colony this year have not passed unnoticed by the Marquis de Vaudreuil . . .

MONTCALM
It would be extraordinary, under the circumstances, if the Marquis de Montcalm, on the basis of what he has heard, did not inform . . . Vaudreuil of his reflections although he cannot suggest a firm project, as he has not been informed of the position of the colony with regards to supplies, nor the number of Canadians and troops of the Marine that may take the field. He can but give vague and generalized advice.

VAUDREUIL
. . . Vaudreuil is always aware of the attention . . . Montcalm gives to present to him the factors involved in the memoir he presents, [and] the motives which guide him.

* * *

MONTCALM
VAUDREUIL

*170. "BERRYER TO VAUDREUIL AND MONTCALM, VERSAILLES, FEBRUARY 10, 1759" (*Lévis Collection*, Vol. 3, pp. 166-70).

The principal object of which you must not lose sight is to conserve at least a sufficient portion of the colony, and to maintain yourselves in it, so that the whole may be recovered when the peace treaty is signed. . . . It is up to you to judge the best means to accomplish this . . . and to keep the English more or less distant from the centre of the colony. . . . In short, you should try and maintain yourselves as best you can in the coming campaign, and await the negotiations which may preserve Canada or operations to rescue it.

*171. "MEMOIR ON CANADA IN WHICH IS EXAMINED 1—IF IT IS IMPORTANT TO CONSERVE IT; 2—IF IT CAN BE DEFENDED SHOULD THE WAR CONTINUE IN 1759; 3—IF IT IS POSSIBLE TO ASSIST IT IN THE PRESENT CONDITIONS, JANUARY 1759" (R.A.P.Q., 1923-1924, pp. 23-29).

FIRST QUESTION

Is it important to conserve Canada?

At all times there have been people who have thought, and perhaps still do think, that it is of very little importance to France to preserve Canada. Some say that it costs the King too much and that expenses will rise. That no profits, or almost no profits, have been made. That in 1755, 1756, 1757, and 1758 the annual expenses have been . . . more than fifteen million which could be better spent in the . . . Kingdom.

Others say that the Kingdom is being depopulated . . . in order to populate an extremely harsh country, filled with lakes and forests, and which often suffers from crop failures. That in the Kingdom there are fertile lands which remain uncultivated. That the commerce with the Indians is not much to talk about and the fur trade cannot last a century. They add that trips to Canada are long, arduous, and dangerous.

A third group contends that in all the wars which we will have with the English, Canada will be conquered, at least in part, which will always result in France being unable to preserve her conquests in Europe.

Besides which, when Canada is well established, revolutions will follow. Is it not to be expected that kingdoms and republics will be formed which will separate from France?

One can see in the "History of New France" by Father Charlevoix [volume 1, book 4, p. 175] that these same objections . . . were proposed to the King's Council in 1631 and were answered in such a way as to lead His Majesty to conserve those vast lands; here are the main reasons:

1—It is certain that if France abandons Canada heresy will be rampant. The known or unknown nations will remain pagans or will adopt the religion of England. So many souls lost for ever! This reflection will strike a Christian Prince.

2—France possesses in North America more territories than there are on the continent of Europe.

We do not as yet know of all the wealth. The better locations are not as yet settled. The glory of the King demands that we conserve so vast a country in spite of the immense expenses . . . ; it is always sad to see enemies growing at our expense. . . .

3—Here one should consider general reasons why it is important to a state to have colonies. It is an error to claim that the Kingdom is being depopulated for the benefit of the colony. One year of war in Europe kills off more men than are needed to populate New France. . . .

How many thousands of men are useless in the Kingdom . . . and in other States? Every year the English gain from foreign countries families which they assist to establish in New England . . . ; there is no country so easy to preserve; maritime forces essential to Old France could protect Acadia and Louisbourg, and we can be sure that if France loses Canada she will need more maritime forces than ever, for the English will become absolute masters of the sea.

It is true that in time these vast lands may become separate kingdoms and republics, but the same holds true for New England.

But how many centuries will elapse first?

Suppose, in effect, that Canada will never be very useful to France . . . does it mean nothing to stop a rival nation from growing, from establishing on the seas a despotic empire and monopolizing all commerce?

The English, once masters of Canada, will necessarily take Louisiana, and the Islands, for once no longer threatened by the inhabitants of Canada, they will concentrate all their forces . . . which for France would be dangerous.

For the same reasons one can be assured that the English will take . . . Mexico from the Spanish, and the Portuguese will feel the effects.

*   *   *

Without knowing all the branches of commerce . . . possible in New France, we can say that the King would lose, and that the trade of England would be increased by more than 150 million. . . .

*172. "VAUDREUIL TO LÉVIS, GENERAL HEADQUARTERS, SEPTEM-
    BER 13, 1759" (*Lévis Collection*, Vol. 8, pp. 106-8).

A very unfortunate event has occurred. At dawn the enemy surprised M. de Vergor who was in command at l'Anse-du-Foulon. They quickly gained the heights and imperceptibly . . . St. John's Road, of which they were in command with at least 5,000 . . . of their troops. . . . I wasted no time in preparing our troops to displace the enemy. . . . Montcalm arrived with the first detachment. I was part of the rear guard, and quickened the pace of the militia troops on my route. I had . . . Bougainville advised, who, in an instant, marched from Cap Rouge with the five companies of grenadiers, two field pieces, the cavalry, and all that he had that was useful. Although the enemy had forestalled us, his position was critical. All we had to do was await . . . the arrival of . . . Bougainville, for while we could attack with all of our forces, he [the enemy] would also be attacked from the rear. But fate was not with us to the extent that the engagement was undertaken too hastily. . . . As a result of this event, this is our present position: 1— We are not prepared to revenge ourselves this evening; our army is too demoralized and we could not rally it. If we wait until tomorrow the enemy will be entrenched in an unassailable position. 2— I cannot, and will not, consent to the capitulation of the whole colony. 3— Our retreat thus becomes imperative. . . .

*173. "BOUGAINVILLE TO BOURLAMAQUE, CHARLESBOURGH, SEPTEMBER 18, 1759" (*Lévis Collection*, Vol. 5, pp. 357-58).

You know . . . the details of our unfortunate adventure; the loss of our general, of the most defensible position in the world, and, I would almost say, of our honour. A man is taken by surprise at l'Anse des Mères. I am at Cap Rouge. The enemy disembarks at midnight; I am only told at eight o'clock. . . . Montcalm . . . believes himself compelled to attack without awaiting my arrival. When I am prepared to take the field the army is routed and the enemy forces attack me. I retreat and take up a position in such a way theat I may take the field if I am so ordered, or make a junction with our army or cover a retreat.

*   *   *

174. "ARTICLES OF CAPITULATION, MONTREAL, SEPTEMBER 8, 1760" (*Constitutional Documents*, Vol. 1, pp. 25-36) .

ARTICLE 1ST

Twenty-four hours after the signing of the present capitulation, the British General shall cause the troops of his Britannic Majesty to take possession of the Gates of the Town of Montreal; and the British Garrison shall not enter the place till after the French troops shall have evacuated it. — "The whole Garrison of Montreal must lay down their arms, and shall not serve during the present war. . . ."

ARTICLE IVTH

The militia after evacuating the above towns, forts and posts, shall return to their habitations, without being molested on any pretence whatever, on account of their having carried arms. "Granted."

ARTICLE IX

The British General shall engage to send back, to their own homes, the Indians, and Moraignans, who made part of his armies, immediately after the signing of the present capitulation, and, in the meantime, the better to prevent all disorders on the part of those who may not be going away, the said General shall give safeguards to such persons as shall desire them, as well in the town as in the country. "The first part refused, — There never have been cruelties committed by the Indians of our army: and good order shall be preserved."

ARTICLE XII

The most convenient vessel that can be found shall be appointed to carry the Marquis de Vaudreuil, M. de Rigaud, the Governor of Montreal, and the suite of the General, by the straitest passage to the first seaport in France; and every necessary accommodation shall be made for them. This vessel shall be properly victualled at the expense of his Britannic Majesty: and the Marquis de Vaudreuil shall take with him his papers, without their being examined. . . . "Granted, except the archives which shall be necessary for the government of the colony."

ARTICLE XXVII

The free exercise of the Catholic, Apostolic, and Roman Religion, shall subsist entire, in such manner that all the states and the people of the Towns and countries, places and distant posts, shall continue to assemble in the churches, and to frequent the sacraments as heretofore, without being molested in any manner, directly or indirectly. The people shall be obliged, by the English government, to pay their Priests the tithes, and all the taxes they were used to pay under the Government of his most Christian Majesty. — "Granted, as to the free exercise of their religion; the obligation of paying the tithes to the Priests will depend on the King's pleasure."

ARTICLE XXX

If by the treaty of peace, Canada should remain in the power of his Britannic Majesty, his most Christian Majesty shall continue to name the Bishop of the colony, who shall always be of the Roman communion. . . . "Refused."

ARTICLE XXXII

The communities of Nuns shall be preserved in their constitutions and privileges; they shall continue to observe their rules, they shall be exempted from lodging any military; and it shall be forbid to molest

them in their religious exercises, or to enter their monasteries. . . .
"Granted."

ARTICLE XXXIII

The preceding article shall likewise be executed, with regards to the
communities of Jesuits and Recollets, and of the houses of the priests of
St. Sulpice at Montreal; these last, and the Jesuits, shall preserve their
right to nominate to certain curacies and missions, as heretofore. — "Refused till the King's pleasure be known."

ARTICLE XXXVI

If by the treaty of Peace, Canada remains to his Britannic Majesty, all
the French, Canadians, Acadians, Merchants and other persons who
chuse to retire to France, shall have leave to do so from the British General. . . . Both the one and the other shall take with them their families,
servants, and baggage. — "Granted."

ARTICLE XXXVII

The Lords of Manors, the Military and Civil officers, the Canadians
as well in the Towns as in the country, the French settled, or trading, in
the whole extent of the colony of Canada, and all other persons whatsoever, shall preserve the entire peaceable property and possession of the
goods. . . . They shall have liberty to keep, let or sell them, as well to the
French as to the British; to take away the produce of them in Bills of
exchange, furs, species or other returns. . . . They shall also have the furs
which are in the posts above, . . . and may be on the way to Montreal.
. . . — "Granted. . . ."

ARTICLE XXXIX

None of the Canadians, Acadians, or French, who are now in Canada,
and on the frontiers of the colony, . . . shall be carried or transported
into the British colonies, or to Great Britain. . . . — "Granted, except with
regard to the Acadians."

ARTICLE XLI

The French, Canadians, and Acadians . . . shall not be forced to take
arms against his most Christian Majesty, . . . the British Government
shall only require of them exact neutrality. — "They become subjects
of the King."

ARTICLE XLII

The French and Canadians shall continue to be governed according
to the custom of Paris, and the Laws and usages established for this
country. . . . "Answered by the preceding articles, and particularly the
last."

*   *   *

VAUDREUIL
JEFFEREY AMHERST

APPENDICES

APPENDIX A
POPULATION STATISTICS

1608	28
1628	76
1641	240
1653	2,000
1663	2,500
1665	3,215
1668	6,282
1679	9,400
1685: 10,725 plus 1,538 Indians	12,263
1695: 12,786 plus 853 Indians	13,639
1706	16,417
1719	22,530
1734*	37,716
1739	42,701
1754	55,009

* Considered the most accurate census.

APPENDIX B
GOVERNORS OF NEW FRANCE

Samuel de Champlain	1612-29
	1633-35
Charles Jacques de Huault de Montmagny	1636-48

Louis de Coulonge d'Ailleboust	1648-51
Jean de Lauzon	1651-56
Pierre de Voyer, Vicomte d'Argenson	1658-61
Pierre Dubois, Baron d'Avaugour	1661-63
Augustin de Saffray Mézy	1663-65
Daniel de Rémy, Sieur de Courcelle	1665-72
Louis de Buade, Comte de Frontenac	1672-82
Lefèvre de La Barre	1682-85
Jacques René de Brisay, Marquis de Denonville	1685-89
Louis de Buade, Comte de Frontenac	1689-98
Louis Hector de Callières	1699-1703
Philippe de Rigaud, Marquis de Vaudreuil	1703-25
Charles, Marquis de Beauharnois	1726-47
Roland Michel Barin, Comte de La Galissionière	1748-49
Jacques Pierre de Taffanel, Marquis de la Jonquière	1749-52
Dusquesne de Menneville, Marquis de	1752-55
Pierre de Rigaud, Marquis de Vaudreuil-Cavagnal	1755-60

APPENDIX C

INTENDANTS OF NEW FRANCE

Jean Talon	1665-68
Claude de Bouteroue	1668-70
Jean Talon	1670-72
Jacques Duchesneau	1675-82
Jacques de Meulles	1682-86
Jean Bochart de Champigny	1686-1702
François de Beauharnois	1702-5
Jacques and Antoine Raudot	1705-11
Michel Bégon	1710-26
Claude Thomas Dupuy	1726-28
Gilles Hocquart	1731-48
François Bigot	1748-60

APPENDIX D

BISHOPS OF NEW FRANCE

François de Montmorency Laval	1674-88
Jean Baptiste de la Croix Chevrière de Saint-Vallier	1688-1727
Louis François Duplessis de Mornay	1727-33
Pierre Hermann Dosquet	1733-39
François Louis Pourroy de Lauberivière	1739-40
Henri-Marie Dubreuil de Pontbriand	1741-60

APPENDIX E

FRENCH MINISTERS OF MARINE: 1669-1760*

Jean-Baptiste Colbert	1669-83
Jean-Baptiste Colbert Seignelay	1683-90
Louis de Pontchartrain	1690-99
Jérôme de Pontchartrain	1699-1715
Conseil de la Marine	1715-23
Jean-Fréderic Phélipeaux de Maurepas	1723-49
Rouillé, Comte de Jouy	1749-54
Jean-Baptiste Machault d'Arnouville	1754-57
Nicolas-René Berryer	1758-61

* The Ministre de la Marine was in charge of colonies.

APPENDIX F

THE CURRENCY OF NEW FRANCE*

It will have been noted that in referring to currency, the documents on the French Régime use the terms *écu, louis, livre, sol* or *sou,* and *denier.* These were the French units of currency in the period under consideration in the present volume. We find, as well, the use of the

* The best account of Canadian currency during the French Régime will be found in *Documents Relating to Canadian Currency, Exchange, and Finance during the French Régime,* edited by A. Shortt.

terms *card money,* *bills of exchange,* and so on. These latter terms are media of currency rather than values of exchange.

It is proposed in the following note and table, to present briefly an indication of the relations of units of French currency one to another, and thereby provide a tentative table of equivalents to English money, as well as an indication of the relation of French money to our current Canadian currency.

A word of caution, however, is an absolute requirement. The intrinsic or metal value of French currency cannot indicate its value in purchasing power *then* or *now.* All that can be given is a very approximate idea of value. It should also be borne in mind that the metropolitan governments of the colonies during the colonial period changed the values and relations of their currencies literally hundreds, even thousands, of times. The table which follows has greatest applicability to the eighteenth century.

TABLE OF EQUIVALENT VALUES OF CURRENCY

Unit of Currency	*livre*	*sou or sol*	*denier*
1 louis d'or	20-24*		
1 English pound	20-24		
1 Spanish dollar or 'piece of eight'	5-6		
1 Canadian dollar	5-6		
1 écu	3-5		
1 livre		20	
1 French franc		20	
1 English shilling		20	
1 Canadian quarter		20-25	
1 sou or sol			12
1 English penny		2	
1 Canadian cent		1	
1 liard			3

* Range due to fluctuating value of currency.

BIBLIOGRAPHY

The most important part of any book is the bibliography. This is not because it indicates the breadth and scope of the readings of the author, but rather because it furnishes the materials for further study.

This note is meant to indicate a *few* of the available secondary works mainly in *English* on the French Régime. Following the note a listing of primary and secondary sources will be found. Each entry is followed, in brackets, by a reference to the parts of this book to which it has relevance.

As was noted in the introduction there is no one really adequate book that may be used as a text for the French Régime. The most adequate, at the moment, is *The Parkman Reader*, a selection of excerpts by S. E. Morison from Parkman's massive *France and England in North America*.

The first two volumes of *Canada and Its Provinces* also provide an adequate coverage of New France. Some of the sections are brilliant, but the work is uneven and characterized by what can only be called *arrière* interpretations.

A more recent general survey of the French Régime has been begun by Gustave Lanctot. His *A History of Canada from Its Origins to the Royal Régime* is but a prelude to several volumes to follow. Dr. Lanctot's work is not marred by so many prejudices as Parkman's.

A readily available, and excellent work on the European background and expansion is to be found in J. H. Parry's *The Establishment of the European Hegemony, 1415-1715*. G. N. Clark's *The Seventeenth Century* and Lough's *An Introduction to Eighteenth Century France* are also superior works. The economic background of French colonization will be found in C. W. Cole's *Colbert and a Century of French Mercantilism*, and Elinor Barber's *The Bourgeoisie in 18th-Century France* complements Cole's work. The intellectual milieu will be found in *European Thought in the 18th Century from Montesquieu to Lessing* by P. Hazard.

The outstanding work on the explorations in New France is that of J. B. Brebner: *The Explorers of North America*. Among the biographies of explorers, that of Bishop—*Champlain, A Life of Fortitude*—and of Delanglez—*Life and Voyages of Louis Jolliet*—are noteworthy. The exploration and settlement of the continent may be further considered by consulting D. G. Kerr's *A Historical Atlas of Canada*.

The early economic history of New France was considered in Biggar's *Early Trading Companies of New France*. Other superior works are those of Innis: *The Fur Trade in Canada* and *The Cod Fisheries*. However, only parts of these works are devoted to the French Régime. One of the more brilliant books on the economic history of New France is G. T. Hunt's *The Wars of the Iroquois, A Study in Intertribal Trade Relations*. The two general texts on the economic history of Canada, Mary Quayle Innis's *An Economic History of Canada* and Easterbrook and Aiken's *Canadian Economic History*, are too generalized to be considered adequate. As yet, the better studies are to be found in monographs and unpublished theses.

The seigniorial system, generally studied as a colonial agency, properly belongs, as well, in the economic section. It is the lack of such orientation that limits the usefulness of Munro's *The Seigniorial System in Canada*, as well as Dorothy Heneker's *The Seigniorial Régime in Canada*. The best work on the seigniorial system is that of Marcel Trudel: *The Seigneurial Régime*; however, its eighteen pages scarcely provide sufficient space for a profound study.

One of the recent trends in Canadian historiography has been the writing of new biographies of the significant figures of Canadian history. With one exception this trend has not extended to the history of French Canada. W. J. Eccles's *Frontenac, the Courtier Governor* stands in lonely grandeur. It will be noted that few biographies have been included in the bibliography. The reason is simple: most are very poor.

Another neglected aspect of the French Régime are studies in social relations. The best, although much disputed, is Guy Frégault's *Canadian Society during the French Régime*. Another very useful work is that of S. D. Clark: *The Social Development of Canada, An Introductory Study with Select Documents*.

Two other excellent works on the French Régime are C. P. Stacey's *Quebec, 1759*, and the first seven chapters of Stanley's *Canada's Soldiers,*

1604-1954. Both works are notable not merely for being specific studies but for their appreciation of the *Canadian* context and influences.

PRIMARY, PRINTED

Atkins, T. B., ed., *Selections from the Public Documents of the Province of Nova Scotia*, trans. B. Curren. Halifax: Annand, 1869. 755 pp. (Parts I to IV)

Boucher, Pierre, *Canada in the Seventeenth Century*, trans. E. L. Montizambert. Montreal: G. E. Desbarats & Co., 1883. 84 pp. (Part II)

Biggar, H. P., ed., *The Voyages of Jacques Cartier*. Publications of the Public Archives of Canada, No. 11. Ottawa: King's Printer, 1924. 330 pp. (Part I)

———, ed., *Les Précurseurs de Jacques Cartier, 1497-1534*. Publications des Archives, No. 5. Ottawa: Imprimerie de l'État, 1913. 212 pp. (Part I)

———, ed., *A Collection of Documents Relating to Jacques Cartier and the Sieur de Roberval*. Publications of the Public Archives of Canada, No. 14. Ottawa: Public Archives of Canada, 1930. 577 pp. (Part I)

———, general ed., *The Works of Samuel de Champlain*. 6 volumes. Toronto: Champlain Society, 1922-36. (Part I)

Burpee, L. J., ed., *Journals and Letters of Pierre Gaultier de Varennes de La Vérendrye and His Sons with Correspondence Between the Governors and the French Court, Touching the Search for the Western Sea*. Toronto: The Champlain Society, 1927. 548 pp. (Part IV)

Canada, Government of, *Censuses of Canada, 1665-1871*. Vol. IV. Ottawa: I. B. Taylor, 1876. 422 pp. (Parts I to IV)

Canada, Public Archives, *Report of the Public Archives of Canada*. (Parts I to IV)

Casgrain, l'abbé H. R., ed., *Extraits des Archives des Ministères de la Marine et de la Guerre à Paris et Correspondance Générale, MM. Duquesne et Vaudreuil, Gouverneurs-Généraux, 1755-60*. Québec: L. J. Demers, 1890. 310 pp. (Part IV)

———, ed., *Collection de Manuscrits du Marechal de Lévis*. 12 volumes. Québec: L. J. Demers, 1889-95. (Part IV)

Casson, François Dollier de, *Histoire de Montreal, 1640-1672*. Attributed to François Dollier de Casson, Priest of St. Sulpice of Paris, 3 Superior of the Seminary of Montreal. Annotated by P. Margry; notes and appendices by J. Viger. Mémoires de la Société Historique de Montréal, No. 4. Montréal: La Minerve, 1868. 295 pp. (Part II)

Charlevoix, S.J., R. P. F. X., *History and General Description of New France*. Translated by J. G. Shea in 6 volumes. New York: J. G. Shea, 1866-72. (Parts I to IV)

Creux, S.J., François du, *The History of Canada or New France*. 2 volumes.

Eds. and trans., P. J. Robinson and J. B. Conacher. Toronto: The Champlain Society, 1951. (Parts I and II)

Denys, Nicholas, *The Description and Natural History of the Coasts of North America, (Acadia)*, trans. and ed. W. F. Ganong. Toronto: Champlain Society, 1908. 625 pp. (Parts I and II)

Dièreville, Sieur de, *Relation of the Voyage to Port Royal in Acadia or New France*, trans. Mrs. C. Webster, ed. J. C. Webster. Toronto: Champlain Society, 1933. 324 pp. (Parts I and II)

Graham, G. S., ed., *The Walker Expedition to Quebec, 1711*. Toronto: Champlain Society, 1953. 441 pp. (Part III)

Grenier, Fernand, ed., *Papiers Contracoeur et Autre Documents Concernant le Conflit Anglo-Français sur l'Ohio de 1745 à 1756*. Québec: Presses Universitaires Laval, 1952. 485 pp. (Part IV)

Innis, H. A., ed., *Select Documents in Canadian Economic History, 1497-1783*. Toronto: University of Toronto Press, 1929. 581 pp. (Parts I to IV)

Jamet, Dom Albert, ed., *Marie de l'Incarnation, Ursulines de Tours: Fondatrice des Ursulines de la Nouvelle France. Écrits Spirituels et Historiques Publiés par Dom Claude Martin de la Congrégation de Saint Maur*. Réédités par Dom Albert Jamet de la Congrégation de France. 4 volumes. Québec: l'Action Sociale, 1935. (Parts II and III)

Kalm, Peter, *Travels in North America*. 2 volumes. Trans. J. R. Forster. London: 1772. (Part IV)

Knox, Captain John, *An Historical Journal of the Campaigns in North America for the Years 1757, 1758, 1759 and 1760*. 3 volumes. ed. A. G. Doughty. Toronto: Champlain Society, 1914. (Part IV)

La Hontan, Louis Armand, Baron de, *New Voyages to North America*. 2 volumes. London: Bonwicke, 1735. (Part III)

Lanctot, G., ed., *The Oakes Collection: New Documents by La Hontan Concerning Canada and Newfoundland*. Ottawa: King's Printer, 1940. 69 pp. (Part III)

La Tour, abbé Louis Bertrand de, *Mémoire sur la Vie de M. de Laval, Premier Évêque de Quebec*. Cologne: Motiens, 1761. (Parts II and III)

Lescarbot, Marc, *The History of New France*. 3 volumes. Trans. W. L. Grant. Toronto: The Champlain Society, 1907-11. (Part I)

Margry, Pierre, ed., *Découvertes et Établissements Français dans l'Ouest et dans le Sud de l'Amérique Septentrionale, 1614-1754*. 6 volumes. Paris: Maisonneuve, 1879. (Parts I to IV)

Morin, Soeur Marie, *Annales de l'Hôtel Dieu de Montréal*. Collated and Annotated by A. Fauteux, E. Z. Massicotte, C. Bertrand. Introduction by V. Morin. Mémoires de la Société Historique de Montréal, No. 12. Montréal: Imprimerie des Éditeurs, 1921, 252 pp. (Part II)

Munro, W. B., ed., *Documents Relating to the Seignorial Tenure in Canada,*

1598-1854. Toronto: The Champlain Society, 1908. 380 pp. (Parts I to IV)

O'Callaghan, E. B., ed., *Documents Relating to the Colonial History of the State of New York*. 11 volumes. Albany: Weed, 1856-61. (Parts I to IV)

————, ed., *The Documentary History of the State of New York*. 4 volumes. Albany: Weed, 1850. (Parts I to IV)

Olier, Jean Jacques, *Les Véritables Motifs de Messieurs et Dames de la Société de Notre Dame de Montréal pour la Conversion des Sauvages de la Nouvelle France*. Attributed to J. J. Olier. Annotated by P. Margry. Introduction by l'abbé H. A. Verreau. Mémoires de la Société Historique de Montréal, No. 7. Montreal: Berthiaume & Sabourin, 1880. 94 pp. (Part II)

Preston, R. A., and L. Lamontagne, trans. and ed., *Royal Fort Frontenac*. (The Champlain Society, Ontario Series, 11). Toronto: University of Toronto Press, 1958. 503 pp. (Parts II to IV)

Quebec, Government of, *Arrêts et Règlements du Conseil Superieur de Quebec et Ordonnances et Jugements des Intendants du Canada*. Volume 2. Québec: E. R. Fréchette, 1855. 650 pp. (Parts II to IV)

Quebec, Government of, *Collection de Manuscrits Contenant Lettres, Mémoires et Autre Documents Historiques Relatifs à la Nouvelle France Receuillis aux Archives de la Province de Québec*. 4 volumes. Québec: A. Coté et Cie., 1883-85. (Parts I to IV)

Quebec, Government of, *Complément des Ordonnances et Jugements des Gouverneurs et Intendants du Canada Précéde des Commissions des Dits Gouverneurs et Intendants et des Differents Officiers Civil et de Justice*. Volume 3. Québec: E. R. Fréchette, 1856. 776 pp. (Parts II to IV)

Quebec, Government of, *Documents Historiques: Correspondance Échangée entre les Autorités Française et les Gouverneurs et Intendants*. Volume 1, (1620-1685). Québec: Demers, 1893. 244 pp. (Parts I and II)

Quebec, Government of, *Édits, Ordonnances Royaux, Déclarations et Arrêts du Conseil d'État du Roi Concernant le Canada*. Volume 1. Québec: E. R. Fréchette, 1854. 648 pp. (Parts II to IV)

Quebec, Government of, *Édits, Ordonnances, Déclarations et Arrêts Relatif à la Tenure Seigneuriale Demandés par une Addresse de l'Assemblée Législative, 1851*. Québec: E. R. Fréchette, 1851. 308 pp. (Parts II to IV)

Quebec, Government of, *Jugements et Déliberations du Conseil Souverain de la Nouvelle France, 1663-1716*. 6 volumes. Québec: A. Coté, 1885-1891. (Parts II to IV)

Quebec, Government of, *Rapport de l'Archiviste de la Province de Québec, 1920-1960*. (Parts I to IV)

Québec, Société Literaire et Historique de, *Collection de Mémoires et de Relations sur l'Histoire Ancienne du Canada: Mémoires sur le Canada depuis 1749 jusqu'a 1760*. Québec: De Cowan, 1840. 207 pp. (Part IV)

Radisson, P. E., *The Explorations of Pierre Esprit Radisson*, ed. A. T. Adams. Minneapolis: Ross & Haines, Inc., 1961. 288 pp. (Part III)

Sagard, Gabriel Théodat, *The Long Journey to the Country of the Hurons*, ed. G. M. Wrong, trans. H. H. Langton. Toronto: Champlain Society, 1939. 410 pp. (Part II)

Saunders, A. G., and D. Rowland, trans. and ed., *Mississippi Provincial Archives, 1701-1740: the French Dominion*. 2 volumes. Jackson: Department of Archives and History, 1927. (Parts II and III)

Shortt, Adam, ed., *Documents Relating to Canadian Currency, Exchange, and Finance during the French Régime*. 2 volumes. Ottawa: King's Printer, 1925-26. (Parts III and IV)

Shortt, A., and A. G. Doughty, eds., *Documents Relating to the Constitutional History of Canada*. 2nd ed. *Volume I, 1759-1774*. Ottawa: King's Printer, 1918. 581 pp. (Part IV)

Têtu, Mgr. H., and l'abbé C. O. Gagnon, eds., *Mandements, Lettres Pastorales et Circulaires des Évêques de Quebec*. Volumes 1 and 2. Quebec: A. Coté et Cie., 1887-88. (Parts III and IV)

Thwaites, G., general ed., *The Jesuit Relations and Allied Documents*. 72 volumes in 36. New York: Pageant Book Co., 1959. (Parts I to III)

Tyrrell, J. B., ed., *Documents Relating to the Early History of the Hudson Bay*. Toronto: Champlain Society, 1931. 419 pp. (Parts III and IV)

Webster, J. C., ed., *Acadia at the End of the 17th Century: Letters, Journals and Memoirs of Joseph Robineau de Villebon, Commandant in Acadia*. Saint John: New Brunswick Museum, 1934. 232 pp. (Part III)

Wood, W., ed., *The Log of the Conquest of Canada*. Toronto: Champlain Society, 1909. 335 pp. (Part IV)

SECONDARY

Audet, L. P., *Le Système Scolaire de la Province de Quebec*. Tome II: *L'Instruction Publique, 1635-1800*. Québec: Éditions de l'Érables, 1950. (Parts I to IV)

Bailey, A. G., *The Conflict of European and Eastern Algonkian Cultures, 1504-1700. A Study in Canadian Civilization*. Saint John: New Brunswick Museum, 1937. 206 pp. (Parts I to III)

Barber, Elinor, *The Bourgeoisie in 18th Century France*. Princeton: Princeton University Press, 1955. 165 pp. (Parts III and IV)

Biggar, H. P., *Early Trading Companies of New France*. Toronto, 1901. 308 pp. (Parts I and II)

Bishop, M., *Champlain, Life of Fortitude*. New York: Alfred A. Knopf, Inc., 1948. 364 pp. (Part I)

Brebner, J. B., *The Explorers of North America, 1492-1806*. Garden City: Doubleday & Company, Inc., 1955. 431 pp. (Parts I to IV)

Burpee, L. J., *The Search for the Western Sea*. Toronto: Musson Book, n.d. 651 pp. (Parts I to IV)

Cahall, Raymond du Bois, *The Sovereign Council of New France.* New York: Columbia University Press, 1915. 274 pp. (Parts III and IV)

Cahiers de l'Académie Canadienne Française, Volume 2, Histoire. Montréal: Pierre DesMarais, 1957. 188 pp. (Parts I to IV)

Carron, l'abbé Ivanhoe, *La Colonisation du Canada sous la Domination Française.* Québec, 1916. 90 pp. (Parts I to IV)

Chapais, Thomas, *Jean Talon, Intendant de la Nouvelle-France.* Québec: Imprimerie S. A. Demers, 1904. 540 pp. (Part III)

——, *Le Marquis de Montcalm, 1712-1759.* Québec: Garneau, 1911. 695 pp. (Part IV)

Clark, G. N., *The Seventeenth Century,* 2nd ed. Oxford: Clarendon Press, 1947. 378 pp. (Parts I to III)

Clark, S. D., *The Social Development of Canada: an Introductory Study with Select Documents.* Toronto: University of Toronto Press, 1942. 484 pp. (Parts II to IV)

Cole, C. W., *Colbert and a Century of French Mercantilism.* 2 volumes. New York: Columbia University Press, 1939. (Parts III and IV)

Delalande, J., *Le Conseil Souverain de la Nouvelle France.* Québec: Ls.-A. Proulx, 1927. 358 pp. (Parts III and IV)

Dalanglez, S.J., *Jean de, Frontenac and the Jesuits.* Chicago: Institute of Jesuit History, 1939. 296 pp. (Part III)

——, *Life and Voyages of Louis Jolliet, 1645-1700.* Chicago: Institute of Jesuit History, 1948. 289 pp. (Parts II and III)

Easterbrok, W. T., and H. G. J. Aiken, *Canadian Economic History.* Toronto: The Macmillan Company of Canada, 1956. 606 pp. (Parts I to IV)

Eccles, W. J., *Frontenac, the Courtier Governor.* Toronto: McClelland & Stewart, 1959. 406 pp. (Part III)

Fauteux, J.-N., *Essai sur l'Industrie au Canada sous le Régime Français.* 2 volumes. Québec: Ls.-A. Proulx, 1927. (Parts III and IV)

Frégault, Guy, *Canadian Society during the French Régime.* Canadian Historical Association Booklet No. 3. Ottawa: Canadian Historical Association, 1956. 16 pp. (Parts II and III)

——,*François Bigot, Administrateur Français.* 2 volumes. Montréal: Imprimerie St. Joseph, 1948. (Part IV)

——, *Iberville le Conquérant.* Montréal: Éditions Pascal, 1944. 415 pp. (Parts II and III)

——, *La Guerre de la Conquête.* Montréal: Fides, 1955. 514 pp. (Part IV)

Garneau, F. X., *History of Canada,* trans. A. Bell. 2 volumes. Montréal: Lovell, 1862. (Parts I to IV)

Gerin, L., *Aux Sources de Notre Histoire.* Montréal: Fides, 1946. 275 pp. (Parts I to III)

Gosselin, l'abbé A., *L'Église du Canada depuis Monseigneur Laval jusqu'a la Conquête*. 3 volumes. Québec: Laflamme, 1911. (Parts II to IV)

——, *L'Instruction au Canada sous le Régime Français, (1635-1760)*. Québec: Laflamme, 1911. 501 pp. (Parts II to IV)

Groulx, l'abbé L., *Histoire du Canada Français depuis la Découverte*. Volumes 1 and 2. 2nd ed. Montréal: l'Action Nationale, 1954. (Parts I to IV)

Hazard, P., *European Thought in the 18th Century from Montesquieu to Lessing*. London: Hollis & Carter, 1954. 471 pp. (Parts III and IV)

Hamelin, Jean, *Économie et Société en Nouvelle France*. Cahiers de l'Institut d'Histoire. Québec: Presses de l'Université Laval, 1960. 137 pp. (Parts III and IV)

Heneker, Dorothy A., *The Seignorial Régime in Canada*. Quebec: Ls.-A. Proulx, 1927. 447 pp. (Parts II to IV)

Henripin, Jacques, *La Population Canadienne au Début du XVIII Siècle*. Paris: Presses Universitaires de France, 1954. 129 pp. (Part III and IV)

Hunt, G. T., *The Wars of the Iroquois: A Study in Intertribal Trade Relations*. 2nd Printing. Madison: University of Wisconsin Press, 1960. 209 pp. (Parts II to IV)

Innis, H. A., *The Cod Fisheries: The History of an International Economy*. Toronto: Ryerson Press, 1940. 520 pp. (Parts I to IV)

——, *The Fur Trade in Canada*. Revised ed. Toronto: University of Toronto Press, 1956. 463 pp. (Parts I to IV)

Innis, Mary Quayle, *An Economic History of Canada*, 3rd ed. Toronto: The Ryerson Press, 1948. 363 pp. (Parts I to IV)

Kennedy, J. H., *Jesuit and Savage in New France*. New Haven: Yale University Press, 1950. 206 pp. (Parts I to IV)

Kerr, D. G., *A Historical Atlas of Canada*. Toronto: Nelson, 1960. 120 pp. (Parts I to IV)

Lanctot, Gustave, *L'Administration de la Nouvelle France. L'Administration Générale*. Paris: Librairie Ancienne Honoré Campion, 1929. 169 pp. (Parts II to IV)

——, *A History of Canada from Its Origins to the Royal Régime, 1663*. Toronto: Clarke Irwin, 1962. (Parts I and II)

LeJeune, R. P. L., *Dictionnaire Générale de Biographie, Histoire, Litterature, Agriculture, Commerce, Industrie et des Arts, Sciences, Moeurs, Coutumes, Institutions Politiques et Religieuses du Canada*. 2 volumes. Ottawa: Université d'Ottawa, 1931. (Parts I to IV)

Lough, J., *An Introduction to Eighteenth Century France*. London: Longmans, Green & Company, Ltd., 1960. 349 pp. (Parts III and IV)

McLennan, J. S., *Louisbourg from Its Foundation to Its Fall, 1713-1758*. London: Macmillan & Co., Ltd., 1918. 454 pp. (Part IV)

Munro, W. B., *The Seignorial System in Canada: A Study in French Colonial*

Policy. New York: Longmans, Green & Co., Inc., 1907. 296 pp. (Parts II to IV)

Myrand, E., *Sir William Phips devant Québec, 1690. Histoire d'un Siège.* Québec: Demers, 1893. 428 pp. (Part III)

Nute, Grace, *Caesars of the Wilderness: Medart Chouart, Sieur des Groseilliers and Pierre Esprit Radisson, 1618-1710.* New York: Appleton-Century-Crofts, Inc., 1943. 386 pp. (Parts II and III)

Parkman, F., *The Parkman Reader*, ed. S. E. Morison. Toronto: Little, Brown & Co., 1955. 524 pp. (Parts I to IV)

———, *France and England in North America.* 12 volumes. Boston: Little, Brown & Co., 1880. (Parts I to IV)

Parry, J. H., *The Establishment of the European Hegemony, 1415-1715.* New York: Harper & Row, Publishers, 1961. 202 pp. (Parts I to IV)

Renaud, P. E., *Les Origines Économiques du Canada.* Mamers: Enault, 1928. 488 pp. (Parts I to IV)

Rich, E. E., *Hudson's Bay Company, Volume I, 1670-1763.* Toronto: McClelland and Stewart, 1960. 687 pp. (Parts II to IV)

Salone, Emile, *La Colonisation de la Nouvelle France.* Paris: Guilmoto, 1905. 467 pp. (Parts I to IV)

Sée, H., *La France Économique et Sociale au 18iè Siècle.* 6 éd. Paris: Librairie Colin, 1958. 197 pp. (Parts III and IV)

Shortt, A., and A. G. Doughty, *Canada and Its Provinces*, volumes 1 and 2. Toronto: Glasgow, Brook and Company, 1917. (Parts I to IV)

Stacey, C. P., *Quebec, 1759.* Toronto: The Macmillan Company of Canada, 1959. 210 pp. (Part IV)

Stanley, G. F. C., *Canada's Soldiers, 1604-1954: The Military History of an Unmilitary People.* Toronto: The Macmillan Company of Canada, 1954. 410 pp. (Parts I to IV)

Sulte, B., *Histoire des Canadiens Français, 1608-1880.* 4 volumes. Montréal: Wilson, 1882. (Parts I to IV)

Tanguay, Mgr. Cyprien, *Dictionnaire Généalogique des Familles Canadiennes depuis la Fondation de la Colonie jusqu'à Nos Jours.* 7 volumes. Province de Quèbec: Eusèbe Sénécal, 1871-1890. (Parts I to IV)

Trudel, M., ed., *Collection de Cartes Anciennces et Modernes pour Servir à l'Étude de l'Histoire de l'Amérique et du Canada.* Québec: Presses Universitaires Laval, 1948. (Parts I to IV)

———, *The Seigneurial Régime.* Canadian Historical Association Booklet No. 6. Ottawa: Canadian Historical Association, 1960. 18 pp. (Parts II to IV)

PERIODICALS

Bulletin des Recherches Historiques
Cahiers des Dix
Le Canada Français
*Canadian Historical Association Report**
Canadian Historical Review†
Review of Historical Publications Relating to Canada
Revue Canadienne
Revue de l'Histoire de l'Amérique Française
Revue Trimestrielle Canadienne
Royal Society of Canada, Transactions

PERIODICAL ARTICLES‡

Adair, E. R., "Dollard des Ormeaux and the Fight at the Long Sault", *C.H.R.*, XIII, No. 2 (June 1932), 121-37. (Part II)

———, "Anglo-French Rivalry in the Fur Trade During the Eighteenth Century", *Culture*, VIII (1947), 434-55. (Parts II and III)

———, "France and the Beginning of New France", *C.H.R.*, XIII, No. 3, (September 1944), 246-78. (Part I)

———, "The French Canadian Seigneury", *C.H.R.*, XXXV, No. 3, (September 1954), 187-207. (Parts II to IV)

———, "The Evolution of Montreal Under the French Régime", *C.H.R.*, XXIII, No. 1, (March 1942), 20-41. (Parts II to IV)

Biggar, H. P., "Cartier's Objective", *C.H.A.*, 1934. pp. 121-23. (Part I)

Burt, A. L., "The Frontier in the History of New France", *C.H.A.*, 1940. pp. 93-99. (Parts I to IV)

Eccles, W. J., "Frontenac's Military Policies, 1689-1698: a Reassessment", *C.H.R.*, XXXVII, No. 3 (September 1956), 201-24. (Part III)

———, "Frontenac and the Iroquois", *C.H.R.*, XXXVI, No. 1 (March 1955), 1-16. (Part III)

———, "Frontenac: New Light and a Reappraisal", *C.H.A.*, 1954. pp. 20-27. (Part III)

Glazebrook, G. de T., "Roads in New France and the Policy of Expansion", *C.H.A.*, 1934. pp. 48-56. (Parts III and IV)

---

* Abbreviated as *C. H. A.* in articles listed.

† Abbreviated as *C. H. R.* in articles listed.

‡ These articles are a selection from English-language periodicals only. The two best sources in French are the *Revue de l'Histoire de l'Amérique Française* and the *Bulletin des Recherches Historiques*.

King, J. E., "The Glorious Kingdom of the Saguenay", *C.H.R.*, XXXI, No. 4 (December 1950), 390-400. (Part I)

Lanctot, G., "Was Dollard the Saviour of New France?", *C.H.R.*, XIII, No. 2 (June 1932), 138-46. (Part II)

———, "The Elective Council of Quebec of 1657", *C.H.R.*, XV, No. 2 (June 1934), 123-32. (Part II)

Lower, A. R. M., "The Forest in New France: A Sketch of Lumbering in Canada before the English Conquest", *C.H.A.*, 1928. pp. 78-90. (Parts III and IV)

Lunn, Jean, "The Illegal Fur Trade Out of New France", *C.H.R.*, XX, No. 1 (March 1939), 61-76. (Part IV)

Morton, A. S., "La Vérendrye: Commandant, Fur Trader, and Explorer", *C.H.R.*, IX, No. 4 (December 1928), 284-98. (Part IV)

Murray, Jean A., "The Early Fur Trade in New France and New Netherlands", *C.H.R.*, XIX, No. 4 (December 1938) 365-77. (Parts II and III)

Preston, R. A., "The Laconia Company of 1629: An English Attempt to Intercept the Fur Trade", *C.H.R.*, XXXI, No. 2 (June 1950), 125-44. (Part I)

Reid, Allana G., "General Trade Between Quebec and France during the French Régime", *C.H.R.*, XXXIV, No. 1 (March 1953), 18-32. (Parts I to IV)

———, "Intercolonial Trade During the French Regime", *C.H.R.*, XXXII, No. 3 (September 1951), 236-51. (Parts II to IV)

———, "The Nature of Quebec Society during the French Régime", *C.H.A.*, 1951. pp. 26-35. (Parts I to IV)

Savelle, M. "Diplomatic Preliminaries of the Seven Years' War in America", *C.H.R.*, XX, No. 1 (March 1939), 17-36. (Part IV)

Stacey, C. P., "The Anse au Foulon, 1759. Montcalm and Vaudreuil". *C.H.R.*, XL, No. 1 (March 1959), 27-37. (Part IV)

Stanley, G. F. G., "The First Indian Reserves in Canada". *Revue d'Histoire de l'Amérique Française*, IV, No. 2 (September 1950), 178-210. (Parts II and III)

Sulte, B., "The Captains of Militia", *C.H.R.*, I, No. 3 September 1920), 241-45. (Parts III and IV)

INDEX

A

Abenaki, 103, 110

Acadia, 11, 100, 103, 105, 106, 142, 143, 144, 145, 146, 155

Administration (see Government)

Agriculture, 2, 25, 26, 31, 47, 53, 54, 56, 78, 111 116, 118, 122, 123, 124 (see also Commerce; Seigniorial system)

Aix-la-Chapelle, Treaty of, 142, 145

Animals, domesticated, 111, 112

Army, 59, 60, 61, 62, 105, 113, 117, 132, 134, 153, 154 (see also Government)

Artisans, 7, 15, 19, 27, 53, 78, 132, 135 (see also Labour)

Asia (see East, route to)

Attorney-General (see Judicial system; Government)

Augsburg, Wars of the League of, 93

Austrian Succession, War of the, 115, 142

B

Bay of Fundy, 142

Bay of the North (see Hudson's Bay)

Beauharnois, Charles, Marquis de (Governor of New France), 104, 113, 114, 117, 123, 126

Beaver, 2, 17, 18, 31, 36, 83, 84, 100, 101, 109, 110, 113, 118 (see also Commerce; Exports; Furs)

Bégon, Michel (Intendant of New France), 99, 104, 108, 117, 138, 140

Bellomont, Earl of (Governor of New York), 98

Berryer, Nicolas-René (Minister of Marine), 151

Bigot, François (Intendant of New France), 126, 143, 148, 149

Bills of Exchange (see Currency)

Bishop of Quebec (see names of bishops)

Bourgeoisie, 35, 36, 79, 105 (see also Commerce; Merchants; Seigniorial system)

Braddock, Edward (British army commander), 143

Brébeuf, S.J., R.P. (see Jesuits)

British-American Colonies, 36, 40, 55, 86, 94, 95, 97, 98, 101, 103, 104, 110, 135, 142, 143, 152

Budgets (see Finance)

C

Caen, William de (Calvinist merchant), 21

Callière, Louis Hector de (Governor of Montreal and New France), 95, 97

Calvinists, 20, 21

Canada (see New France)

Canadians, character of, 104, 131, 132, 133, 134, 135, 140

Canadiens (see Canadians, character of)

Cape Breton Island (see Louisbourg)

Card money (see Currency)

Carignan-Salières Regiments, 53, 54, 60, 73

Cartier, Jacques, 1, 3, 4, 5, 7, 8, 9, 10, 20

Casson, Dollier de (Sulpician, historian), 27, 28, 29, 79

Cataraqui (see Fort Frontenac)

Cayuga (see Iroquois)

Censitaire (tenant farmer) (see Seigniorial system)

Census (see Population)

Chabanal, S.J., R. P. Noel (Jesuit mystic and martyr), 32, 35 (see also Jesuits)

Champigny, Jean Bochart de (Intendant of New France), 96, 117

Champlain, Samuel de (Explorer, coloniser, governor), 1, 2, 3, 10, 12, 13, 14, 16, 20, 21, 24, 49, 78, 94

Charlevoix, S. J., R. P. François-Xavier (French historian), 81, 111, 131, 151

Charters, 2, 3

China (see East, route to)

Church (see Roman Catholic Church)

Cod (see Fish)

Colbert, Jean Baptiste (Minister of Marine), 42, 50, 54, 56, 58, 60, 62, 68, 70, 73, 81, 90

Colonial rivalries, 1, 24, 27, 36, 40, 41, 55, 80, 93, 94, 96, 97, 108, 110, 142, 143